My path is universalism.
My words are for all those
who walk this broadest of all
paths.

Second (revised) edition published in 2018
First published in 2016
by GlobalQuest Enterprises
PO Box 89, Warburton VIC 3799, AUSTRALIA

© Keith Simons 2016

This book is copyright. Apart from any fair dealing for the purposes of private study, research or review permitted under the Copyright Act 1968, no part may be stored or reprocuced by any process without prior written permission. Enquiries should be made to the publisher.

National Library of Australia
Cataloguing-in-Publication data:

Simons, Keith, 1949-,
Elucia/Keith Simons.
ISBN 978-0-9758365-1-4
1. Simons, Keith, 1949-.

Front cover: original hand drawn mandala artwork by Keith Simons

ELUCIA

A Multidimensional Biography

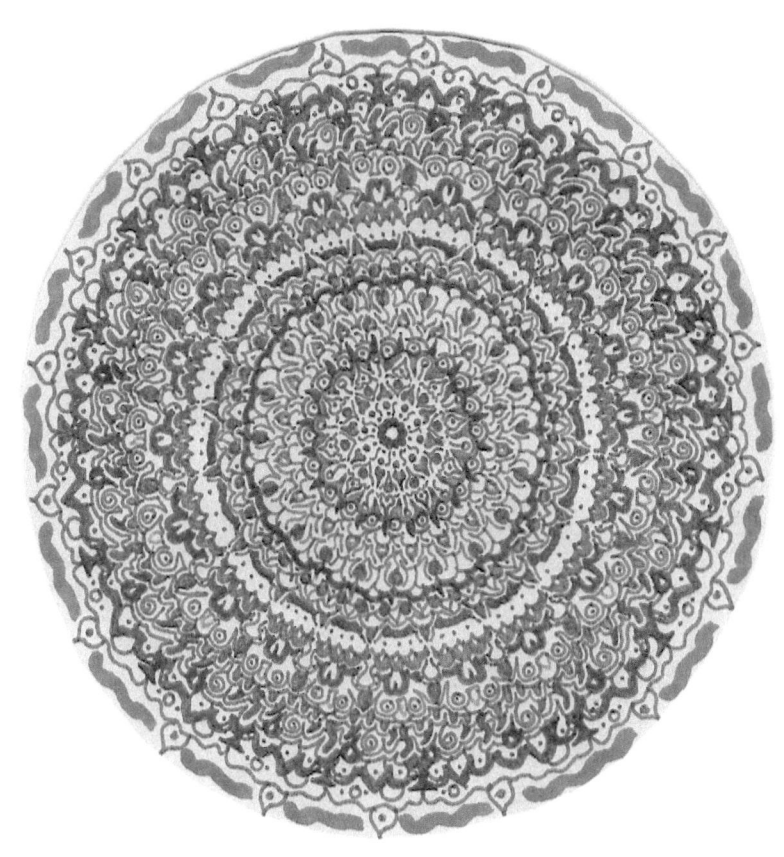

KEITH SIMONS

I dedicate this book to my wife Leanne and to Rudolf Steiner, whose 9-volume series of lectures 'Karmic Relationships' was the sublime inspiration behind this work.

Contents

INTRODUCTION 9

PROLOGUE 11

PART 1
BIOGRAPHY

1 Event Horizon   19
2 Separation   21
3 Disperson   25
4 Biological Life   29
5 Humanoids   32
6 Human Beings   36
7 Intervention   39
8 Evolutional Shift   44
9 Karmic Relationships   48
10 Homo Spiritus   58

PART 2
EVOLUTION

11	Wisdom	*67*
12	Purpose	*69*
13	Gathering	*72*
14	Equality	*77*
15	Healing	*80*
16	Experiment	*83*
17	Homo Biotech	*87*
18	Splitting	*89*
19	Consciousness	*92*

PART 3
INNER WORK

20	Deep Listening	*99*
21	Interest in Others	*102*
22	Meditation	*104*
23	Openness	*106*
24	Alignment	*109*
25	Honesty	*113*
26	Compassion	*117*
27	A Strong Heart	*119*

PART 4
THE GREAT WORK

28 The Implicate Order   *123*
29 Soul Clusters   *126*
30 Planetary Shifts   *129*
31 Fifth Dimensionality   *133*
32 Restoration   *135*
33 Transcendence   *139*
34 The Great Overcoming   *141*
35 A New Language   *144*
36 Reconciliation   *147*
37 Transformation   *149*

EPILOGUE   157

AFTERWORD   167

ADDENDA (2ND EDITION)
Responses to questions from readers of the 1st edition

On Language   *171*
On Identity   *176*
On Awakening   *181*
On Christ   *185*
On Technology   *190*
On the Etheric Christ   *193*

Introduction

This is a evolutionary book. The author is translating, as best he can, a biography of someone who is no longer embodied. It is therefore a different type of collaboration. The soul of the disembodied one shall remain nameless except for a spiritual name especially chosen for this work.

Elucia, as he/she shall be known, has information, messages and inspirations vitally important for humanity in the twenty-first century, as Elucia too prepares for future reincarnation.

Even if the reader benefited from a small portion of this book it would serve a significant purpose.

The scribe urges all who have the opportunity to read this 'biography' to do so with an open mind and heart.

Then it will speak to you. It will address a deeper part of your own soul's knowledge, even if in the form of vague feelings or intuitions.

We are living through challenging times. Individually and collectively we are constantly bombarded by information. This is indeed an information age.

What is presented in these pages offers an alternative perspective on our place in the universe and our home planet. It touches on many of the vital issues of our times within a universal, evolutionary context. The information and messages contained in this work will build slowly and, if you allow it, respond to the question, 'What is my purpose and who am I?' One way or another you will benefit from a careful reading of this book.

As has occurred in this 2nd edition, further questions can be answered in new editions of the book. In this way the work can interact and evolve with new responses to the events and happenings of our time.

Prologue

Words will come of their own accord, in a fashion. This will be an experiment for both of us: the biographer and I, who was once known by many names whilst embodied. From long long ago I understood my mission. The writer of this biography had a similar mission. That is why he is sanctioned to attempt this work. Our destinies are interwoven. The story of human evolution is complex. It far predates earthly existence. So does my biography. It is not easy to express this in ordinary human language so you will need to read between the lines.

Let us first become aware of a fact that can be challenging to absorb while incarnated as a human. As souls we are all interstellar beings. My mission is therefore as an interstellar being. When a human individual incarnates in a particular place on Earth a special identification is forged. When that person evolves into an adult and travels here and there, a wider identification with place occurs. Do you see how an embodied soul identifies with the physical, and as one experiences more of the external environment, how that alters one's perspective, identity and relationships? Now imagine passing over the threshold of death and entering into a spatial field so vast that there seems to be no limit to one's identity. This happens when a soul passes through the gate of death: identity expands and transcends. To what degree depends on the type of identity experienced whilst embodied. As will become clearer, individuated souls develop in vastly different ways as they evolve trans-dimensionally.

To understand my biography it is important to explain some essential facts. The way that individual souls evolve is complex and non-uniform. This can be easily observed even within the physical earth conditions prevailing at any time. Therefore human individuality is unique in its unfoldment. Within this individual soul evolution, networks of relationships are formed. If we can imagine a 'beginning of intention' it can provide a basis for understanding what is important. A 'beginning of intention' can take us into our own deepest wisdom, and more, to our mission as souls. This mission in its essential character belongs to a *universal impulse of intention*. It is the primary impulse for your universe: an interstellar force that rays throughout your entire cosmos, your immeasurable galaxies and all your sun-stars.

You may ask, 'What is this primary intention?' What is vital to understand is that primary intention separated itself into many secondary rays, and separate beings became custodians of these rays. Imagine one clear light birthing a multitude of colours, all intimate expressions of the one Light. Each soul therefore belongs to a particular ray, but behind that, to the one original universal impulse. In the most essential sense of our identity, all souls are emanations of the One Being that experienced the one intentional impulse. And yet individual souls simultaneously belong to particular intentional rays. It is here that our primary missions come into play, hidden for humans by the development of individuated thinking. That is until an awakening occurs that is occultly embedded within each human soul.

What can be said about the one primary impulse that expresses like so many child-rays destined to rejoin the original parent? This primary impulse had an intention. The best way to reveal this is by analogy. Picture a creative individual who experiences an impulse to create something. Imagine this as exceedingly beautiful: full of harmony, relationship, creativity, inspiration, wisdom, intelligence and love. And imagine that this impulse intends for the image to become manifest: to become embodied. If this is to be inspired into reality beyond a mere image, a principle that cannot be changed must be permitted: that principle is freedom. Once the One becomes many, the principle of freedom becomes variefied and differentiated. If it wasn't for this principle of freedom we would have a clockwork universe.

The choice to become an individuated, separated entity is an original free choice in personal evolution. If we comprehend that this choice is associated with a universal, interstellar mission we can ask, 'What types of missions are then set in motion?' More so, 'What mission is my being connected to and what essential intentional impulse is my primary soul signature?' My biographer and I belong to related soul rays.

You see, various ray streams are related in complex webs. For example, my ray stream and mission is the same as my biographer's but then further choices in evolutionary time-space create other dimensions of sub-rays, like shades of colours. So to begin with, the ray that is my primary intentional impulse belongs to what can be described as cosmopolitan, universal or interstellar. It is the same with my biographer and that is why he is sanctioned to transmit this, my biography. This is the primary ray impulse that we both respond to.

Many souls are intimately connected with each other because secretly they belong to the same intentional stream and this has evolved through space-time in cosmological and galactic manifestations. This doesn't only apply to human beings. Human incarnations are only one type of evolutional expression of these various interstellar rays. It will begin to become clear if you contemplate deeply how you are karmically linked to other souls, both incarnate and discarnate, and by extension to other incarnate species, as if dancing to a mystic tune that can only be heard by awakened souls. In cosmological terms this is the tip of the iceberg. You are linked by virtue of spiritual qualities that are common and attract souls to each other again and again.

Our biographies therefore begin in the mists of early evolutional time, when what some of your present physicists refer to as an event horizon occurred, erringly understood as the Big Bang. What is misleading about the Big Bang model is that it wasn't the actual beginning, only *a* beginning. Imagine any creative phase of a human incarnation; it can be perceived as both an ending and a beginning. Before the beginning there

PROLOGUE

was another preceding phase. We only see as far back as the earliest horizon within our capacity, rather like looking at the horizon when facing the ocean, knowing there is something beyond what we can see. Hence our biographies only began at the beginning of a particular event horizon, in terms of that event.

For all useful intentions my biography begins at our cosmological event horizon.

PART 1

BIOGRAPHY

1 Event Horizon

I was without name and body. I was a part of my Creator, and I as Creator freely chose to separate from Creator, giving birth to myself, so to speak. At that moment in space-time, Creator allowed a vast separation of Source into myriads of separate constituents. This was not done in a random or arbitrary way. There had been a type of conference within the pleroma, if you can imagine a conversation with oneself. Humans do this and Creator did this too. There were many different potential streams co-existing in Creator's mind. They all needed to be honoured. These many streams or rays were, to begin with, like voices or thoughts in Creator's mind. They had not separated yet in any externalised way, akin to a chrysalis lava in which the past caterpillar awaits future emergence as a butterfly.

There is a middle term that is neither past nor future but contains the essence of both in a kind of suspended state. I, as an individuated entity, hadn't yet emerged. Nor had any other entity. There was only Creator having a big conference within.

This could not go on forever. The whole evolution of creation would come to a standstill. With the image of the chrysalis, you don't see it, but a transformation is happening. This can't go on forever, or there would be no external butterfly. The butterfly must burst forth out of the chrysalis in order for externalisation to occur. So it is with the event horizon. Nature presents, for those who have eyes to see it, a microcosmic template for us to understand the beginning of our universe.

The so-called Big Bang was the event horizon when the first outpouring of separation occurred. That is when we all began as particular rays of intention. This was the first dimension of separation from Creator, from Source. This was the first interstellar manifestation.

2 Separation

Energy as we know it belongs to a cosmologically ancient Source. It is Creator's intelligence and power expressing intentionally. It is exceedingly difficult to describe this energy source in modern language but if you imagine the power of your Sun and multiply that by all the zillions of stars in the universe, with the heat, power and light that emanates into the deep darkness of space, you can intuit a sense of this beyond mere concepts. When this point of unimaginable Source first exploded and dispersed into your early universe, intelligence itself separated into various rays. These were the first primordial ray streams of Divine energy, and were the first level of cosmic hierarchy, closest to Source as they still are, and always must be. This could only change if the entire Universal manifestation became reabsorbed into Source, with the free choice to once again re-emerge as a fresh universe. Here we have a hint at how our own present universe emerged. These first original differentiated rays had potentially complementary missions and orientations, also purposes. And all souls that followed in the wake of this chose to align with one or another of these rays.

From where did these souls come from? They were birthed, so to speak, by the Rays themselves, but before that happened there was a great internal council. This is not easy to understand because the freedom to choose was within each Ray or stream of separated intelligence. What you need to grasp is that souls already existed within One Source. They existed as different threads in the tapestry of Creator's consciousness, but had no separate external existence. When Source birthed the first layer, if you will, of separated intelligent streams or entities, myriads of souls were attracted to the various streams. But having been so attracted another layer of inner council debate ensued. Souls could still change their orientation and join another Ray. This was considered a vital phase for the future evolution of your universe because once your universe further evolved it would be difficult to change alignment and allegiance. This first dimension of separated Rays was in your later myths represented as the hierarchy of Gods and Goddesses. The Source is not considered as a dimension, being beyond all categories.

My personal biography as a separated Being begins here. It is here that I chose to separate from my parent, the Source, and devote myself to a particular mission and purpose. This same missionary stream attracted many souls, destined to further separate in ever widening evolutionary expansions as the One Archangelic Ray further diversified: the primary focus behind all the diversified expressions. It is this focus that is the Universal archetypal impulse. As such it doesn't belong only to one Sun but to all suns, and that is its character: it is

Interstellar. It has brought a multi-universalistic impulse into your particular universe, and therefore belongs to what is known as the eternal pleroma. It is also that which is known as omniscient (all seeing), omnipotent (all powerful) and omnipresent (eternal). The qualities of this ray you know as unconditional love, harmony and grace, but beyond all else, relationship. The Buddhist teacher Thich Nat Hahn coined the word 'interbeing'. It captures the relational quality of this ray, its quality of consciousness, understanding and feeling which harmonises all, and becomes an external representation of the original unity of Source before it diversified. My devotion to this quality and its evolutional unfolding began a long time before my soul (monad) incarnated into humanoid clothing. For millennia it helped to oversee the evolution of Intelligence in its various streams as energy transformed into ever more dense manifestations. Although from a physical human perspective these manifestations would be viewed as abstract: essentially formless and immaterial.

The first universal hierarchy consisted of beings as far from physical incarnation as conscious beings can be. Their capacity to hold together harmoniously was intact, but their freedom of expression was extremely limited from a human perspective. Within this missionary stream the principle of freedom existed as an underlying depth impulse. The twin propensities of harmony and freedom prompted a further council between souls. It is important to understand that the use of the word 'soul' in the context of these early evolutional phases should not be confused with the strong sense of individuality now experienced by humans. These souls were interconnected parts of each other, and yet could communicate as if separated and united simultaneously. This council engaged in a strong debate about how to increase the principle of freedom. The only way to do this was to further separate and individuate variable, inherent potentialities of the ray. In inter-ray councils it was agreed that all the rays had to likewise separate and individuate. Henceforth another level or dimension of separated rays was birthed in what was essentially a repeat of the original dispersion. This became the second dimensional hierarchy.

3 Dispersion

Not all souls or spectrums of the Rays chose to die and be reborn into another dimension of existence. At a certain point in the process I made that choice. To reach the status of human being, or any other embodied soul, such choices to evolve into ever increasing tangible or solidified manifestations have to occur. With each further externalised transition there is a greater degree of complexity, but also a greater freedom of expression.

Please understand what I am describing here relates mainly to my own biography. The evolution of your universe is tremendously complex. For example, other rays and their dispersion into multiple sub-rays, and how they evolve further, is of a matrix-like complexity that is far beyond the scope of ordinary human language, knowledge and relevance for this particular biography. Significant to understand is that there have been four such major dispersions, and humanity is on the threshold of the fifth. But more of that later.

The first dispersion was from Source to the first hierarchy and dimension of suns (stars). This was eventually followed by the second dispersion into the second dimension, symbolised and manifested from Suns into planets, comets and other dark matter. The third dispersion into the third dimension was from dark matter to living organisms. The fourth dispersion into the fourth dimension was from living organisms (biological life) to humanoid physical biological beings. The fifth dimension will be to spiritually awaken humans. This successive dispersion of dimensions was simultaneously a cooling of the immense heat that was generated from outbursts from Source.

To return to the dispersion into the second dimension, from Suns to dark matter overseen by intelligent rays, it must be understood that conscious beings that are dispersions of Source can simultaneously be in different dimensions. We are by nature trans-dimensional beings. From Source into dual dimension then into three-dimensionality was an evolutional expansion of vast importance. It was necessary if the process towards physical life was to be completed. At the phase of stellar reality nothing existed but suns. There were particles and gaseous elements, but no coalesced matter except suns (stars). This was the state of your early universe which later coalesced and formed planets as the universe cooled. The shift into the second hierarchy involved the choice of some souls to accompany the shift into solidified dark matter. Planets would after all become crucial as future crucibles for biological and human life. Dark matter is the cauldron within which life can emerge into biological forms. I, together with companion souls, chose to follow the ray stream into this third hierarchical dimension with particular intentional impulses. But we were not alone. We were joined by souls who were aligned with quite different intentional impulses. I was focused on my mission of retaining the impulse of harmony within diversity, of knowledge of our origins and interstellar identity. At that time I engaged with my present biographer, and many others who were to share a general common destiny, even down to the present earth time. Our mission though was becoming increasingly diversified and, if you can picture it, specialised. When eventually the time came to transition from the second dimension into the third, from dark matter into biological life, missions became especially diversified and very, very, complex. Biological life was imagined from the beginning as extremely diverse. Think of all the levels and complex diversity of biological life forms on your planet alone. Cooling creates radical changes in the chemistry of the universe. The cooling of the universe is therefore an alchemical process, and the Creator is the original alchemist.

So how does the spectrum of biologically diverse species contribute to the Divine Plan? For make no mistake, there is a Divine Plan, although the word 'plan' is somewhat inadequate. 'Vision' is closer to the reality. Every biological life form has its sacred purpose when considered with fullest vision. The words 'ecology', and even more, 'biological diversity', point to an essential principle: harmony within diversity. Your entire universe is an example of this principle. This is the Grail of universal comprehension. The evolution of diversification enlarges the principle of freedom within diversity, at once gloriously expanding and simultaneously challenging, because the more things expand and diversify the greater the challenge of holding onto principles of freedom and harmony within expanded diversity. An organisation with three or four people which expands to a large organisation with many people, can illustrate how intimacy and emotional connection (warmth) meets this challenge with more and more elements of formality, objectivity and uniformity. If from Source, the intention was to have a uniform harmony (a bit like a Swiss watch) then your universe would be radically different from the one you exist in. There is no freedom of authentic diversity in uniformity. Demonic forces would desire such uniformity for your universe and world. I shall explain about malevolent forces at a later time. So, rays entering into the second dimension of evolution were diversifying, and also the mind streams accompanying them.

4 Biological Life

The missions of the various streams now became far more specialised. Dark matter belongs to a broad spectrum, from minute particles to large solids such as planets. Your recent earth-bound sciences have discovered in Quantum mechanics how broad this spectrum is. I separated from other soul forces at this stage of cosmic evolution and focused especially on the solar system that you now inhabit, but with a role to also attend interstellar councils where representatives of the many ray streams came together to debate larger cosmic concerns. Simultaneously other souls were focusing on other matters relating to galactic or other solar systems. This had already become exceedingly complex. There were already life forms existing in other solar systems and galaxies long before biological life began in your sun system and on your planetary home. All of these were experiments in Creator's mind, set in motion based on different essential principles. These various experiments needed to be at vast distances from each other so as not to easily interfere and overly disturb the natural evolutional processes underway. Nonetheless gatherings of representatives did occur from time to time: galactic councils that eventually formed an officially sanctioned Galactic Federation. As for my biography, it is our particular solar system experiment that is important, as this was especially relevant to my choice of mission. Do you realise that this is true for all who exist within your system? There is nothing random in this. You have chosen to be a part of this particular cosmic experiment because to one degree or another you are attracted to the essential principles that govern your system.

The Archangelic hierarchy (referred to as Angelic by human choice, although they are really solar or sun beings) that governs and oversees the second dimensional activities of dark matter are especially involved in the mineral activities and welfare within your system, and especially your home planet. Although a certain aspect of consciousness identifies with the mineral realm, it is all part of the One: the great pleroma. Many beings chose to remain in this role and didn't transition into the third dimension, that of biological life. Consider the mass of sub-streams that were engendered as this transition occurred on an intergalactic scale. You need to grasp a picture of this in order to appreciate the magnanimous, immense complexity of this universal evolutionary transition. Galaxies already existed in the early universe but they were like infants forming their own identities. In reality they were 'shaping' according to their particular intentions. They formed clusters of galaxies attracted to each other by virtue of sympathetically aligned rays or intentions. This was already vastly complex in its total panoramic movement, a type of plasma reality consisting of forces that were solar and therefore not dispersed into other dimensions. As a microcosmic example of the transition into second dimensional dark matter, think of your sun and moon. The Sun is the plasmic bearer of light and warmth that can only illuminate dark matter, in this example, your moon. Lunar light only exists because dark matter exists, vis-a-vis your moon. Expand this model to the entire universe and you will begin to grasp the enormity and deep significance of this evolutional transition from the first dimension of solar reality to the second of dark matter. Dark matter would be literally dead matter, of no significance whatsoever without the prior existence of the solar dimension. For the consciousness of Source this required another great dispersion of itself into myriads of sub-channels. For me, this led to choosing first and foremost to align with the cosmic experiment that uniquely belonged to your particular cluster of galaxies, then to your galaxy known to you as the Milky Way, and then to your particular solar system, and later as you shall see, to your planet. So it is with all who incarnate on your home planet.

Why did I choose such? This question is intimately aligned with a core aspect of Creator's intention and the sub-variations emanating from it. This intention regards how it is possible for Spirit to incarnate into matter. In this context matter is to be considered in its full meaning, that of inorganic or dark matter, and that of organic matter that evolves into biological life, especially including humanoid physical existence. The further intentional goal is that conscious humanoids, entirely encased in physical bodies, can, as in a circle, return to at-one-ment with Spirit as embodied stellar beings: beings of the stars. This was a mighty passion for me. I was quite aware of the incredible immensity of this task.

5 Humanoids

When the moment arrived to choose to transition from second to third dimensional existence, from dark matter to biological life, I eagerly agreed. There was another massive universal evolutionary development, another tremendous dispersion, and my choice to align with a particular galaxy came into increased force. I had already aligned with a particular galaxy cluster and the consequent development of dark matter within that galaxy.. Now I had to choose what particular galaxy to focus upon. I was already intimately involved with your galaxy, even within the cluster.

What happened with this next phase was a less personal focus on the cluster and a more committed focus on your particular galaxy. The development of biological life within your galaxy became a major part of my mission as a step towards the future of humanoid embodiment. In your sense of earth time these phases can only be counted by billions and trillions of years.

Of course, for non-physical souls, earth time has no meaning. Without a finite body, time has a completely other significance. It is true that a kind of death-rebirth occurs whenever there is a transition from one dimension to another, but this is never an ending, rather a change. With a collection of souls similarly configured as I, we worked with the necessary development of organic life within your galaxy. It is of no arbitrary account that I then further chose to incarnate into humanoid form when the transition from third to fourth dimension occurred. Such transitions into humanoid embodiment did not originate on your home planet. Individual souls do not undertake these transitions as collectives, but clusters continue to exist, as they do macro-cosmically. I was not the first to become incarnated into a biological entity. Nor were my early incarnations into humanoid forms. The experience of incarnating into a biological form when this has never happened before in this universe is beyond description, but I can try and hint at a few things.

When the dispersion to leave the non-biological dimension and enter into any type of biological embodiment occurs, there is a great separation and dissolution of awareness, consciousness and memory, and what you know as forgetfulness sets in. This is because the particular biological, physical embodiment has its own limited laws. This was the first time I experimented with such a loss of memory, knowing that when this particular embodiment dies I will once again remember my soul, the interstellar soul that I am, and my greater mission. The incarnation into essentially simple biological entities was a way to adapt to the transition. This process also took billions of years in your present earth time reckoning. I had to evolve into ever increasing, more complex biological entities, with each greater biological development a way of adapting towards an eventual incarnation into a humanoid birth. Whenever I passed through what has been referred to as the gate of death, I would re-awaken, understand my greater mission and prepare, with assistance, for my next incarnation. Do you see how in this way no incarnation into any biological form or any circumstance can be judged simply? Every incarnation is a step in a vast evolutionary saga with an underlying purpose. So eventually I began to experience incarnational biological lives, until my first humanoid incarnation. This was the transition from third to fourth dimensional existence. When a soul is deemed ready to take on a humanoid embodiment it marks another tremendous evolutionary shift, and a massive step closer to fulfilling Creator's intention for your particular universe, solar system and home planet.

Again I had to slowly adapt to this new stage of development. At this stage all aspects of the multi-dimensional evolutionary processes, rays, streams and sub-streams have become so complex, it is impossible to describe. But the essential intentions are still playing throughout the entire universal symphony. The principle of freedom is now developing into vastly more potent capacities. When early humanoids entered the planetary earth home of your solar system they were not as physically embodied as in later evolutionary times. These times have been lost to your ordinary knowledge, although there are many remnants in myths and indigenous stories. Your history is quite recent in terms of humanoid existence within your solar system. I entered humanoid incarnational history as one of those who were in the vanguard of this transition, but only in regards to your planet. Other humanoid beings already existed within other ray streams in other parts of your galaxy and other galaxies, but very significantly not as physically or atomically dense as on your home planet. This was foreshadowed all along. It was my choice with its greatest freedom and yet greatest risks and obstacles. This experiment, focused towards an eventual spiritual embodiment on your home planet, was always my passion and commitment.

6 Human Beings

To reach the fourth dimensional phase of humanoid embodiment on your planet was a tremendous step in evolutionary terms. It followed billions of years and countless embodiments in mineral, plant and animal species until my soul had adapted to the brilliant intricacy of a human being. It now becomes fascinatingly complex. In order for human beings to evolve towards fifth dimensional spiritual embodied consciousness, it was necessary for some human incarnations to be especially aware of who they really were. A biological human alone means little more than an advanced animal. This is not to disparage any biological creature, but to make clear that all incarnations are part of an evolutionary march towards a particular vision within Creator's mind. The important thing to understand about a biological human is that there is an inherent capacity that offers opportunities to evolve in ways that are truly amazing. I'll tell you why. For more than any other reason, a human organism contains intellectual capacities that lend themselves to cosmic intelligence. But this capacity is also a potential trap. From the very beginning of physical humanoid life on your planet, it was necessary for there to be advanced humanoids who would guide the species towards the fifth dimension. It was decided that for this to occur there needed to be some intervention from other humanoids that were developing in other parts of your galaxy. These humanoids were like ray-cousins who had deviated long ago into other directional streams. They were powerful and intelligent, but not as physically dense or biologically sophisticated as human beings. They were alternative types of humanoids who were close enough to your planetary beings to be able to survive within the early planetary environment. This was happening long before the evidence discovered by your present sciences. Their presence on your planet was not a simple matter of a benevolent gesture of helping evolution along. It was more complicated than that. They had their own subjective needs to consider.

I mentioned the galactic federation earlier, and it was due to such a great council that something remarkable happened. The decision for ray streams to evolve separately enough to not disturb each other was not an absolute fixed principle. It could be modified under certain conditions. Co-operative intergalactic evolution happened too, but this was generally within first, second and third dimensional existence, with an ever-decreasing capacity as the universe evolved through these dimensions. With the transition from third to fourth dimensional life in your solar system, from biological life to humanoid incarnation, the need for a 'Grand Galactic Council' was recognised. If evolution were left to its own devices on your planet, human beings would still be in a very primitive state, even now. What was about to happen was not for the first time: an intervention to speed up the cosmic process.

7 Intervention

It was decided to send an intergalactic presence to earth with a mission to accelerate the evolutionary process. I was not a part of the intergalactic council, but I was involved. No one present in a human embodiment throughout your planetary history has been a member of this council, and their presence on your planet has only ever been intermittent. I only speak of them as pure breeds, not as interbreeds. For all of humanity are interbreeds, to one degree or another.

When physical incarnation became possible, entire new sets of natural laws came into effect. Of these, what you refer to as genetic codes was a biological method of passing on information and reproduction. Remember that humanoids didn't only exist on your home planet. Genetic processes were common throughout the universe, but with different orientations or, in other words, differing codes. These variable codes naturally had varying outcomes. The wonder of this biological genetic dimension was that genes could be mixed or mutated. How this should be accomplished on your planet was a huge topic that occupied the intergalactic council for some considerable time. Some members of the council belonged to particular ray streams that had specific concerns, one could say, of a self-serving nature. Others were more altruistic in their thinking. The leading figures of the council were closer to Source than the others, but they were aware of the principle of freedom that was not to be violated. Their role was to guide, not dictate.

At this time, I was discarnate more than not. I had already incarnated a number of times into this advanced biological animal that was the predecessor of Homo Sapien, early human. I was invited to the council occasionally as one of the representatives of my particular ray stream. This was significant for a number of reasons. My free choice made long before, to belong to this solar system and planetary mission, had rendered me biologically adapted to a degree vastly beyond the capacity of the other inter-stellar council members. I was chosen along with others to consider proposals that were being seriously contemplated. The nature of these proposals was focused around an experiment in genetic mixing that was to accelerate evolutionary processes on your planetary home, especially those of the humanoid. These interstellar council members were already very advanced in certain aspects. They were less biologically condensed and more ephemeral than earth humanoids. They were yet far more second and third dimensional, if you will, and less incarnated into the fourth dimension. This meant, among other things, they were wiser and more powerful by far than even the wisest earth humanoids. They had capacities that were almost God-like, compared to human beings even in your own time, but they didn't have the capacity to incarnate as biologically and physically. So it was needed that some volunteers would be prepared to incarnate as females, and interbreed with selected intergalactic council members and others from their realms that were considered especially suitable. This was what was being suggested to me and others belonging to our mission and ray stream. Those who agreed would become an advanced sub-race on planet earth. Some others and I agreed to be a part of this development. The intergalactic council members then decided on different sub-stream projects. The sub-stream I was to be aligned with had a specific evolutionary intention of developing inner soul consciousness in ways that were essentially free of strict religious or political confinements, although words like religion or politics were yet to be invented. But there was foresight into the types of social structures and languages that would come about in due course.

Language at that time was entirely pictorial, and intergalactic communications were in the form of telepathic images, something like seeing things as they really are. They were easily and immediately understood. My missionary intent was to further the evolutionary development of humanoids towards the fifth dimensional outcome of the truly spiritual biological human. That was the vision and driving force, the source of universalism. If I interbred as a humanoid female and gave birth to a more advanced type of humanoid, this being a part of a breeding program that within my sub-stream alone would account for hundreds of hybrid babies, a new sub-race, then in time I could incarnate into such a body, and take an important role as a guide and leader. In this way I was to give birth to my future selves. The breeding program was then separated into sub-streams under the guidance of intergalactic teams and occurring in different geological locations around the planet, each sub-stream with its orientation and particular set of goals. There were disagreements as to how to undertake some of these missions, so it was eventually decided that different experiments should be conducted as far apart as possible on the planet's surface ,with a high degree of autonomy and lack of interference.

It was known that souls who were destined to incarnate into humanoid embodiments through time would be able to choose the sub-streams they wanted. This is difficult, but let me try and picture this for you. For souls to evolve towards healthy fifth dimensional beings it would be necessary to experience various types of incarnations. Those who, like myself, had already experienced an array of non-human embodiments and had progressed by choice to humanoid incarnation, at first mammalian and ape-like, who accepted to be in the first wave of hybrids, and whose mission was firmly focused on the great mission of evolving towards Homo spiritus, realised in the discarnate realms between embodiments that there were important elements within each sub-stream.

These sub-streams were the origin of our distinct races and sub-races. The origins of the different races belong to hybrid mixes of galactic and humanoid, but realise that souls are free to incarnate among these diverse racial streams.

I have incarnated among a number of these streams, but not as many as my biographer. Our multi-dimensional teachers, mentors and friends guide the choices made, for we are aligned to those clusters that especially resonate with the primary ray we chose to dedicate ourselves to. Very special relationships are made and cultivated over vast eons of time, even billions of years, and echoes of these ancient relationships continue to resound into the present time.

8 Evolutional Shift

We are nearing what is known as the middle section of the fourth dimensional human story. The first phase spanned tens of thousands of years, yet a blink in universal evolutional time. Neanderthals were early hybrids, but not the earliest by a long way. Nonetheless, they were quite successful. Some hybrid subspecies died out quickly. This is a challenging topic, related to intergalactic differences and in some cases, strong disagreements. But unlike Star Wars films, intergalactic differences rarely became actual manifested wars, and in the rare cases when this would occur, it would be resolved quickly. The weakness here is that intentional streams are granted freedom to co-exist, and we humans inherit many divergences which subsequently play out in our fourth dimension. This was already happening in the early phases of your hybrid history. The clashes were instinctive and fuelled by primitive survival impulses, but also other fundamental qualities inherited from inter-dimensional breeding programs. Therefore, some subspecies were more naturally aggressive than others. Some were more naturally curious, and some more inclined towards beginnings of intellectual growth.

Within dense biological conditions, now mixed with new powerful genetic capacities, a quantum leap occurred that brought with it a platform on which greater forces of harmony and discord would play out. It was known that this would happen, and was viewed as a great opportunity and a great risk. This cauldron of mixed contrasting energy streams generated both catastrophic and brilliant consequences, and we are yet intimately involved in this experiment of awe-inspiring proportions. It happened as predicted that those subspecies better adapted to our planetary home would survive at the expense of others less well adapted, but remember we are only referring here to the level that is genetically incarnating. Those sub-streams that died out, for instance, created a need for those souls to choose other types of embodiments, and this caused many difficulties, but also created new openings for growth. For instance, many souls were not well equipped to incarnate into unfamiliar types of racial embodiments than those they identified with and were accustomed to. All this took place over tens of thousands of years in its strong developmental phase.

Until about twelve thousand years ago a situation had been reached, with occasional galactic visitations and interventions, when the major racial types that would henceforth dominate, had been largely settled. Neanderthals had long since disappeared. Homo sapiens, as you now know yourselves, had with various sub-streams or races become the dominant humanoid species. This introduces what can be known as the middle phase of human evolution, when a startling new development began.

What happened was an intervention, not to do with interbreeding, but an actual cosmic event in the form of a comet crashing into your planet. This was a calculated event agreed upon with much trepidation by a special intergalactic council and galactic follow up council. If the second phase was to be initiated, a drastic change in planetary conditions was required. The experiment that your planet is, needed a change in environment, and in the type of balance among existing creatures. Things had got out of hand. The balance was incorrect. Thirteen thousand years ago, many large mammals suddenly became extinct, including some remnants of humanoid subspecies, and amidst tremendous climatic changes only the strongest human strains would survive, which meant the genetic pool became immensely strengthened.

Many souls were ready for this advance. They longed for better incarnational vehicles, and agreed with the councils for this to occur. Without this shift, and it was a shift in many senses, the evolutionary progress towards a fifth dimensional spiritually awakened human would have stalled. Your earth scientists have evidence of something catastrophic happening around that time, but have no idea what it really represented or its complexity.

This middle phase of human development birthed your first great civilisations, yet they too remain hidden in the mists of time. Are you realising how souls were cultivating, so to speak, human evolution? Tracking it according to their increasingly individuated soul developments, the stage was set for karmic streams and relationships to unfold that were more sophisticated and complex than ever before.

One feature that now emerged was certain hierarchies that were shadowy imitations of interstellar hierarchies. One hybrid stream took its impulses from a hierarchy that on your planet evolved into Royalty and Priesthood. This separated into a number of sub-streams. One such sub-stream took root in what is now Asia, another in Africa, and yet another in Northern Europe. These had genetically imprinted impulses added onto original galactic interventions, by way of intermittent galactic visitations.

The cosmic model for this stream was the Solar ruler now known as Christ by many of your people. Royalty and priesthood would diverge into two separate sub-streams of this model, one more secular the other more spiritual. Both these sub-streams developed and co-existed with other primary ray streams now solidifying into increasingly sophisticated karmic manifestations, for example the shamanistic stream.

What you know as culture really has its earthly roots in this time: roughly twelve thousand years to about two thousand years ago when another quantum shift occurred.

These evolutional shifts were indeed happening at shorter and shorter intervals as evolutionary development accelerated. Historical time was and is speeding up. Evolution itself was and is vibrating at ever-faster rates.

9 Karmic Relationships

Two thousand years ago I was involved in a discarnate council of souls passing in and out of earthly incarnations. This was when the relationship with my biographer became far more intimate and intense. We decided that as far as possible, we should incarnate at alternate times, but stay connected. We belonged to an increasingly clearly defined cluster of souls, working in a particular way and with a particular intention. This intention was aligned with a much greater mental acuity than many experienced human souls had developed.

Forms of communication were now present that allowed for vastly enhanced sharing of information, knowledge, feelings and experience. It was possible for there to be some incarnations that were extremely advanced, compared to the masses. Forms of writing had been developed a few thousand years before this, but now had advanced into the type of script that better paralleled human ability to comprehend quite complex thought forms. At the time of Buddha, and then of Jesus, two further interventions occurred that would bring spiritual impulses down into evolving human embodiment. It is not my purpose here to depict these two momentous occurrences, but rather to reveal what choices were made by many souls, including my biographer and myself, during those six hundred years. These choices were of great import for the future. In order to clarify this, allow me to explain a few matters.

There are different modes of human learning and growth in regards to karmic relationships. Two of the primary modes can be distinguished as simultaneous embodied learning and sequential embodied learning. A prime example of simultaneous embodied learning is when souls embodied at the same time form an important bond, resonating consciously on multi-dimensional levels, including the spiritual. Such significant karmic relationships can also occur sequentially. A prime example being when souls, deeply karmically connected, pick up on each other's work and further it, without actually being embodied at the same time.

You may ask, what about partial crossovers? When souls deeply connected choose to work together sequentially, brought about by various complexities, but considered to be a more effective way to further evolution, it would also be realised that time together in the discarnate dimensions would be necessary. One soul is coming into incarnation and the other going out. This arrangement is not absolute but overall, through evolutional time, it happens this way more often than not. It was considered by my biographer and myself to switch from simultaneous to sequential incarnations two thousand years ago, at the time of Jesus being on your planet, and with a couple of short incarnational cross-overs, this has been so until the present time. This is not so significant in regards to the two of us alone, but is an example of a particular mode of karmic relationship that became increasingly significant over the past few thousand years. Our karmic relationship had become more refined and defined as it passed through evolutionary dimensions. We belonged to the same Ray. We were related by intention, and as we passed into human incarnations we kept meeting in incarnate and discarnate spaces until around 600 BC, when we met again as embodied souls, but of quite different ages. I made a deep impression on my biographer in the manner of an elder to a student, but over time we became friends, recognising an empathetic resonance that was deeper than our respective ages. He was an artist, I a philosopher, but we communicated with a profound sense of awakened consciousness.

When we both passed over the threshold as discarnate souls, he some time after me, we attended a soul cluster council that focused on the tremendous changes that were occurring on our home planet. It was foreshadowed that this process of change would herald another vital quantum leap some 500 years ahead, in earth years. We studied how this transition could best be influenced in terms of karmic relationships that were especially at the vanguard of human leadership. This is how relationships were revealed in their subtler interactions. It was seen that groups of souls were better suited to adapting to particular phases of what you refer to as history. This process of adaptation had become more individuated through time, and had reached a point whereby souls who had previously incarnated together were less able to effectively do so. The complementary learning and evolving that occurs in strong karmic ties does not necessarily become easy when souls are developing with increasingly individuated temperaments, interests, affinities, sympathies and antipathies. Details become more significant as humans individuate. Differences that hardly mattered once can become tensions later. This was so between my biographer and me. As discarnate souls we were closer than ever, but as incarnated souls we realised we would clash and divert each other from our main work. On the other hand we realised that by incarnating sequentially we could be attracted to each other's work, and with subtle influences from other related dimensions, what you know as the spiritual realm, we would build on each other's research, and this we have done and are still doing. This biography is a continuation of that mission. It is an example of what is happening among many souls who have strong karmic bonds. And it is what was beginning to be understood in ever-clearer ways in the discarnate realms and shared in councils at that time.

When Jesus incarnated therefore, I was present, but not my biographer, and I was powerfully attuned to his great solar mission. He was not only a representative of the solar realm, but also a member of galactic and intergalactic councils. There have only been relatively few souls who have had so-called triple membership or involvement who have then chosen to incarnate into a human embodiment on our planet. My own status was not as this, but I was a recipient of the knowledge passed on. All the authentic old mystery initiation schools stretching back thousands of years were involved in these councils. They were always attempting to bring the greater interstellar intentions, visions and wisdom into manifested human understanding, experience and actions. It was hence a natural affinity I had with Jesus and his main disciples. I am not at liberty to say who I was at that time, nor of anyone throughout time. It is absolutely unnecessary to know such superficial details in the context of this revelatory biography.

The knowledge imparted at that time, only a few years duration, was of a nature that was revolutionary. Jesus was a radical revolutionary, make no mistake. The Christ impulse was connected to the purest interstellar ray. Its character was Universal and Interstellar in the profoundest sense. Those who encountered this ray through the human vehicle of Jesus were profoundly changed. Christ through Jesus became an archetype, a model for the future Homo spiritus. This in effect was acceleration, as indeed every time when it is deemed necessary to further evolutionary processes on your planet.

This inter-dimensional intervention never obliterates the principle of freedom, and a better way to perceive this is to recognise the fact that you exist in a multi-dimensional and interstellar universe. Planetary life is not separate from cosmic life. In terms of individuated souls and groups of souls, we are not separate. Your business is theirs and theirs is yours.

My own evolution took a quantum leap two thousand years ago. My biographer had taken such a leap some six hundred years earlier, but not of the same magnitude. We realized that by leapfrogging each other sequentially we could better further our common goal and mission. When I passed through the gate of death in the early part of the first century AD, the two of us met in the discarnate realm with other souls with whom we were both strongly bonded. This engendered an atmosphere of intense communication.

The increased individuation of human beings sat alongside a distancing from the universal impulse that had now been boosted by the event of Christ through Jesus. To place this event in a larger context, many other souls had been vehicles for the Christ impulse, which has been and is known by many other names. It is the impulse of universal harmony, wisdom, love and peace, and most importantly a primary re-cognition of true stellar identity. In other words we are all star children.

As history can reveal, some of these interstellar incarnations had tremendous impact, especially for the collective evolution of humanity. The lives of such illuminated humans became legendary. Myth mixed with truth to create stories that are pictorial representations of interstellar principles, and seeds for future manifestations. It was clear that Christ Jesus and the interstellar impulse would inspire future incarnations in ways that would be far more complex than ever before.

For the previous two thousand years the tribal communities scattered about the globe had slowly moved towards settlement. New technologies were inspired and invented, leading to forms of agriculture that allowed commerce to thrive. Trade, politics and religion mixed in countless ways. It was a volatile blend of elements evolving in two opposing directions: away from spirit towards materialism, and towards embodied spirit with its downflow into mind and matter. Although there had been sophisticated civilisations before this, they had been far less materialised and physical.

What is important to grasp is that formative forces are met by deformative forces that have always been active in your universe since the event horizon. From the early universe, when primary intentions began to separate into various ray streams, two diverse movements began. One movement consisted of all of those rays that had a primary intention to remain cooperatively engaged for the welfare of the universe, with the aim of evolving towards spiritually conscious embodiment. The other movement had an intention towards individuation, and therefore separation, but without regard for the welfare of the universe, and with no aim towards eventual conscious spiritual embodiment. These two movements essentially needed each other, but only if the secondary forces were subsumed by the primary ones. This did not happen. This must happen if your solar system experiment is to succeed.

The final exteriorisation of this evolutional process is the dense materialisation and physicality of your planetary state of being. When I received the teachings of Christ through Jesus, the remembrance of my mission became re-clarified and empowered. I took this across the portal of death and worked with other soul friends on a vision for the future. This was governed by the soul who had been Jesus, along with other greatly evolved beings, some who belonged to galactic and intergalactic realms. It was foreseen how I would reincarnate, but I then left this vision behind and re-entered the solar realm with fresh understanding and enthusiasm. It was understood that the way ahead could not continue to follow the old ways of conquest. Bringing new culture and spiritual regeneration to people through conquest had to be replaced by new intellectual and artistic means.

By the time of my next reincarnation, a few hundred years after Jesus walked the earth, I was ready to embody in a very different way than ever I had before. Rome was the cradle of Western civilisation. Literacy had become a real force, at least for the elite who were more educated, but I knew that the Word would become mightier than the sword, and inspired language would be for future generations, not only the few who would benefit in my own embodied time span. My biographer realised this too, as we both attended councils that envisioned and intentioned the future evolutionary streams in just such a manner. But he would follow, and as has occurred ever since, we are always led to each other's writings, and in this way build on each other's work.

This happens, of course, among many deeply connected souls. The process of souls weaving in and out of incarnations, in connected karmic relationships both interpersonally and in groups, working with the same or related ray impulses, has become more refined and focused. Such group missions have created a different collective unfoldment to the old mystery schools. What is important to understand is not all the complex varieties of group workings but the contrast between them as a whole, and the mass of disintegrating and contaminative counter influences brought about by materialistic and non-spiritual thinking. My work in the twentieth century, building on my biographer's from the eighteenth, and many other influences from within our soul cluster, was especially related to this great dichotomy between benevolent and malevolent forces. They were manifesting in ever-greater proportions and threatening the evolutionary experiment on your planet. New forms of incarnational group work needed to be initiated, mirroring as far as possible the discarnate councils already alluded to. These new types of collective efforts are ongoing and crucial. They represent the seed pictures of a spiritual human society that would be a giant step forward, and the fulfilment of at least a portion of the vision emanating from Source. This process would lead, if successful, to a drastic turn-about from the human hierarchies operating in your world at this present time. The changed incarnated hierarchies guiding your world societies would become approximate replications of intergalactic and interstellar harmonies. This would fulfil the maxim 'as in heaven so on earth.'

I am working with tremendous focus within my present discarnate capacity, within an especially formed interstellar council, to penetrate into those who can be ever stronger incarnated workers, bringing new innovations to the great work of individual, collective and societal transformation. This is happening, but simultaneously the forces of self-interest and narcissism are resisting and pouring their energies into increasing their destructive and deformative actions. This is the Armageddon of your Christian mythic symbolism.

The hope rests on two major principles. One, that all those working towards harmony and peace, despite wayward inner tendencies, are aligned with light in the most literal of ways: in other words, with cosmic love, wisdom and intentionality. Second, the forces of separation and self-interest are by virtue of their non-alignment with cosmic forces of Life, destined to self-destruct and fall into oblivion. Ultimately this is a game with only one winner, but that can only lead to another experimental game. For it should be understood that this is an eternal creative process beyond ordinary human comprehension. The entire universe is evolving, and at the heart of this is a mystery that even Source or God doesn't understand. This is the mystery of Being, of Life.

10 Homo Spiritus

The intentioned evolution that has manifested as your civilisation always had a great risk of identification with whatever is external to Source. The further along the pathways towards matter and into biological and physical life, the greater the risk of exclusive identification. Inclusive identification with matter and biological physicality can be integrated with metaphysical and spiritual forces. And yet the embodied experience is compelling, to an extent whereby culture, language and experience are easily thought to be the sole domain of physical and material life. All references to living and dying are of sensory and intellectual processes. These trends into the jaws of Mammon, the whale of materialism, are so powerful that only great interstellar forces can supply a counter-force and orientation. Those souls and clusters of souls that have not yet fallen into the whale's belly are the hope that your planetary evolution can reach its divine potential. Of greatest importance at this time is the outcome of the transition that you are passing through. This transition has reached a critical phase in the evolution of your planet, as you know, but you don't know how significant this is in an interstellar context. Your planetary evolution is not an isolated occurrence with little or no impact on the universe as a whole. Your planetary experiment is unique. Every experiment is unique in its own way, but yours is so in a very special sense. There is no other planet as densely embodied as yours. There are others that harbour biological life forms, but not like your planet. Your solar system is placed specifically and intentionally at the outer edge of an outer limb of your galaxy, just so it is possible for life to evolve as it does on your planet. It has evolved over billions of years. Can you fathom the tragic outcome of this experiment failing?

Human beings are now separated in their consciousness from each other at the widest abyss ever. Homo sapiens are actually separating into two entirely different species. I tried so hard to make a difference when last incarnated, but met few who were as dedicated as I. Why was this? The temptations of embodied existence are massive. There are many souls who, although their missionary zeal is strong, continue to be caught in webs of temptation, losing their focus and clarity. This was happening to increasing numbers of souls throughout my previous many incarnations. It is heartbreaking to observe souls, who have great potential, slip away from their missionary focus and literally lose their way. When such souls pass through the gate of death they experience intense remorse. It is not only for themselves that they experience remorse but for all living beings, and for what it creates in the discarnate realms. The entire interstellar evolution is a layered type of energy and everything: biological life, dark matter and conscious intentionality, are interpenetrating streams of energy. When incarnated souls become mired in deformative thoughts and actions, without redeeming and transforming these energies so that the primary mission can shine forth, then the corrective measures in discarnate dimensions are in effect distractions and wastages, from a greater interstellar perspective.

My dedication and focus is even now unwavering. The traumas humans experience are pale shadows of the remorse experienced by souls who have literally slept through a human incarnation. This is a generalisation, as the entire situation as with all others is tremendously complex and variable, but the truth contained in this account contains a warning and a wake up call.

Too many human incarnated souls exist in a deep coma-like state. My attempts to awaken souls during my previous incarnation fell far short of my intention. This was realised late in that embodiment, and I understood that more was needed in the transcarnate realms. There I could meet with others, and transform energies on subtle levels, before sending down refined streams of energy to those who are incarnated where they can be received as improved ways of working. For behind all these workings is the question, 'What will wake up not just a few here and there but many: so many that a revolution in evolutional direction occurs?'

The word, revolution, is entirely appropriate, because when stripped of its superficial associations it means to turn around. It is this 'turn around' that must happen if your planetary experiment isn't to fail to one catastrophic degree or another. Indeed, because of the primary principle of freedom, many past experiments have failed. Whatever happens, life will go on. Karma is playing out and karma is interactive. In other words relationships in the fullest sense of the word are integral to karma.

Freedom and karma are as two snakes that become forever entwined. Karma without freedom would be like a game without choice: you can exercise your capacity to freely choose, and even though your freedom is limited by karma, the exercise of freedom at your disposal can make a great difference. This is the cutting edge of my main teaching now.

Those who I have established soul connections to, and are furthering the work towards the possible transition into fifth dimensional life, not just individual embodiment, but spiritual culture across your entire planet, must realise that freedom can be directed within the karmic aura that envelops your physical embodiments in ways that can truly make a significant contribution. This is my way of encouraging you to face your wayward karmic tendencies, and recharge your efforts for the sake of your planet and the entire universe. You are at the conscious microscopic end of a universal drama. I hope these words are penetrating and configuring your minds in ways that deeply matter beyond what is obvious to your physical senses.

The time is ripe on your planet for a new type of language. Language too has evolved, always. A language or use of language that doesn't evolve becomes a hindrance. In this way books, including my own, whether written by my own hand or transcripts of talks, need to be understood but not repeated like mantras.

Understand below the level of actual words. Now you must create a universal language accessible to all seekers after higher truths, and all those who have the potential to awaken. You must universalise your consciousness. It must be revealed how we are all interstellar beings. It must be communicated and shown how we are all in this drama together.

The new leading edge sciences occurring on your planet, with our hidden help, must be linked with metaphysical and spiritual insights and accessible revelations. Revelations lead to revolutions.

You must be patient yet courageous. Forgive your own wayward tendencies, but be strong in the choices you make with the freedom you have. The identity as human beings that you have inherited from a long past of ever increasing embroilment in matter and physicality now needs to sublimate, as the two snakes of freedom and karma evolve towards the future Homo spiritus.

What is happening now is unprecedented. The flow down into your planetary biosphere from intergalactic and galactic rays and from your own Sun, has never been so potent. Once again there is a great risk involved with this. Power can corrupt and become usurped by those who are motivated by self-interest. When the voltage is increased, both benevolent and malevolent agencies take advantage.

What is happening on your planet is a not a strict dichotomy between forces. They are entwined in complex formations. This entanglement is where portals of hope exist. For instance, when a ray of wisdom, love or compassion enters into a darkened space, seeds are planted that can be watered and cultivated. The alchemy of energies always involves entanglement.

The hope you can have as incarnated humans in the twenty-first century is justified, but tempered by the risks that freedom of choice naturally presents. My role in this unfoldment is inspired by remembrance of my mission, and what it is founded upon. If you are reading these words you are related to this and to me. You can be certain that our paths have crossed and re-crossed in intricate webs over vast eons of time as we continue the great work.

PART 2

EVOLUTION

11 Wisdom

The questions of uppermost importance for you now should be related to this great work and mission. So let us review this work and mission and consider what may be appropriate questions. Let us remember that we are intimately related to Source, no matter what symbol or name you know it by.

Source is the primary element of your universe and yourselves. Source is wise, intentional, purposeful, harmonious and mysterious. We shall explore these words. For this I call on Source to transmit through me. But realise that these primary stellar qualities also exist latently in you.

By wisdom is meant something quite different from the normal intellectual cleverness of non-spiritual consciousness. What you refer to as atheism is actually a rejection of Spirit, and hence a rejection of the primary element of individuated selfhood. This is unwise no matter how cleverly expressed.

Wisdom is an inherent quality that shines forth when surrounding layers of exteriorisation have been seen for what they are, and consciousness in its natural and infinite beingness recognises itself.

Goethe pointed towards this when he used the words 'natura naturens', the nature of nature, but we need to extend this to the entire universal creation, and beyond to Source. Wisdom is the capacity to distinguish essence from substance, and to understand the relationship between them. This is an indication, a pointer.

Please reflect meditatively on this.

12 Purpose

Intentionality and purposefulness are related terms. Source 'intentioned' this universe into existence. The event horizon burst into creative rays, as intention. This intention naturally gives rise to the innermost sense of purpose.

As incarnated humans you can experience this sense of supreme purpose, beyond all superficial and manufactured imitations. Imitations are limitations, and only foreshadow the real. This supreme sense of purpose is Source intending this universe to exist and thrive, motivated by a grand vision. This vision, as I have stated a number of times, is to manifest spiritually conscious and harmonious biological beings.

This vision is the prime intention emanating from Source, and engendering the sense of supreme purpose which is the natural state of universal harmony. It is an interstellar model exemplified by the awesome spectacle of harmonious intergalactic existence, now able to be fathomed by your earth instruments in ways that offer a glimpse into the true nature of your home universe.

The mysteriousness of Source can only be revealed and understood as a Supreme Mystery. You must become humbled by this self-evident truth as an experience, not merely as a concept.

The question arising from this 'indication' is, 'How am I as an individuated human being to discover my portion of this great work and mission, and to recognise my sense of purpose as authentic?' How did I recognise such when incarnated?

We bring traces of memory and inherent capacities into rebirth. These traces and capacities vary in strength from soul to soul depending on many factors, but especially the development of spiritual qualities. When a soul re-enters a human body, all cognitive memory is lost, but not obliterated. Inherent faculties are present too, but in simple form. The way these two aspects of self unfold, memory and inherent capacities, relates to the environment and how it interfaces with a growing person. In my case, it was always a matter of playing an important role in your planetary evolution.

When such inner capacities have been developed over many incarnations and transcarnations, the inherent qualities are ripe for awakening within a current embodiment. So it was for my previous incarnation. It wasn't that I easily discovered my great work and mission, nor re-engendered my inherent capacities or empowered memories. Rather my inherent capacities were finely enough developed that my choices led me in the direction foreseen before birth, more or less. It was a gradual unfolding, and not until my thirties did I really become clear as to my mission and purpose. This was a beginning more than an ending, as my mission evolved up until my passing through the gate of death. This is a 'work in progress' for me, and all developing souls.

How is this significant to you who may still be seeking your purpose?

Firstly, understand that everything matters even if matter is not everything. Building a strong multi-dimensional entityness is of paramount significance in evolutional terms. Understand you have already evolved to a tremendous degree to become a human embodiment. Your physical embodiment is a potential manifestation as a carrier of Spirit. This is a most remarkable potential.

Every effort, therefore, towards developing your spiritual awareness enhances the awakening of your inherent capacities, many that may have lain dormant or never even awoken. It is the same with memory. We are also capable of building and developing new capacities, so it is a combination of the awakening of inherent capacities, and developing new capacities.

The ultimate purpose belongs to Source. The individual is just discovering ways to express that purpose in a personal form.

13 Gathering

Now is the time for you to begin to replicate our discarnate councils. This is happening, but needs to spread further and deeper, into the bowels of earthly hierarchies that are pale, shadowy imitations of the actual galactic and intergalactic hierarchies. I tried to set something in motion when last embodied and there are and have been numerous other noble attempts to do this across your world. Let us therefore delve a little into what a council could and needs to look like.

It is no arbitrary gathering. Only those who have a sincere inner connection with the ray of universalism, compassion, wisdom, and the evolutional mission towards the fifth dimensional outcome of spiritualised embodiment are invited, with the exception of observers who can benefit.

Firstly such a council is inclusive. Every council member attending has a right to actively participate and contribute, and the freedom to passively observe if felt to be more appropriate. All participants are present because they share a concern for the welfare of all, and for the future. We are the harbingers of the future.

There are 'clearing' practices before communications get underway. These practices are intentions to remove any wayward tendencies in mind and emotion.

There will be one or more senior members well equipped to know when the time is right to proceed. An overview of the topics under consideration would be presented by those who are best equipped to present, based on their particular fields of work.

The motivation for this council is to consider the best ways to advance the mission. The mission is simply everything that furthers the processes required to transition from fourth to fifth dimensional incarnational life.

In your worldly terms, this model can be re-translated into language more accessible to people who are still transitioning. The Dalai Lama's gatherings offer an excellent example of such an earthly replication. Scientists of all kinds, psychologists, sociologists, politicians, religious leaders and spiritual people, gather in an atmosphere of mutual respect and intelligent desire for ethical understanding. When this type of council happens on your planet, within your universities, parliaments, and corporations, and in all other sectors of your societies, you will be well on the way towards transforming your world. For this to happen, individuals need to undergo fundamental shifts of consciousness. The inner-outer exchange as well as the interchange between individuals and groups is therefore of paramount importance. Not only this, but remember that in transcarnate councils, inter-dimensional exchanges are implied. The replication of such on your planet would involve greater councils whereby representatives of all sectors gather together. In that more advanced model, participants are aware of an inter-dimensionality that transcends the obvious presence of those present. An inter-dimensional contribution or involvement is invited, recognised and acknowledged at such gatherings. An example of this already happening is in indigenous gatherings where their ancestors are invited, and understood to be actual living energies beyond any superficial ritual.

Where does such a movement begin in the lives of individual incarnated people living on your planet now?

Every moment offers opportunities on one level or another or in one way or another. It was my strength to forge an intention to not waste any moment. This is my gift to you. It allows me to be of service in ways that would not be possible if I allowed temptations to lead me astray. This focused capacity didn't come easily, but I can assure you that it is possible.

My previous six incarnations have been especially significant. My next will be too. From ancient mystery schools to my present transcarnational state, there has been an unbroken focus on being an effective agent of the ray that is my guide. This ray is the voice of the Supreme Being who is my parent. It is so for everyone, but largely unrecognised.

The recognition that we are God's children, properly understood, is the portal through which you can join the movement that has as one of its primary aims the establishing of councils as I have indicated. Your United Nations and parliamentary democracies try to unconsciously imitate this archetypal template.

The ray that the indigenous peoples belong to was, and is for a few yet, naturally closer in their very natures to respecting such councils. The experience of connectedness is at the heart of this understanding. The indigenous ray was set apart from other sub-streams from the beginning of the hybrid breeding programs. This ray belongs to galactic beings that felt a simpler and more natural evolution was preferred to the more sophisticated and technological capacities of other sub-streams.

Again, remember as souls, many of you have incarnated in different sub-streams or races over eons. The streams can now interchange with each other, and must do so if your planetary evolution is to reach fifth dimensional status. Indigenous people had already reached an aspect of this; they were already spiritualised human beings, but without the expanded consciousness and individuality of other races.

The evolutional harmony possible on your planet must integrate the best qualities of all these rays and sub-streams. Your Harmony Festival was a wonderful attempt to do just that, and the transcarnate realms were delighted. The soul that was Uncle Bob is with us now and has shared much with us already. The indigenous stream is evolving by contact with other streams, and at best combines energies in a truly inspiring way. We here are well pleased with your efforts, both of you, and all who chose freely to contribute.

This was a variation of what I tried to do too, but in my case it was far more limited to those whose incarnational embodiments were European and Balkan. This was for reasons largely out of my control. I tell you this so you can glimpse how changing conditions now offer much more expansive opportunities. I urge you to feel universalism in the core of your beings. The way ahead is both fraught with resistances and obstacles, but also wonderful opportunities that have before never been a part of your planetary situation.

(footnote: The Warburton Harmony Festival, 2014 featured indigenous cross-cultural and inter-spiritual events. The late Yankuntjatjara Elder and traditional custodian of Uluru, Uncle Bob Randall, was a key participant and guest of the Festival.)

14 Equality

All forms of equality are signs that evolutional embodied life is moving in the right direction. For example, gender equality is more significant than meets the eye, but equality in this sense doesn't mean uniformity, rather it takes into account differences and relationships between co-existing biological entities. It is an equality that allows for entire systems to thrive. What your words such as 'ecology' indicate is a bio-diverse environment. Understand that you dwell within a bio-diverse galaxy and universe. Therefore, equality indicates respect for the bio-diversity of planetary life.

Humanity as a whole is attempting to transition from third to fifth dimensional consciousness without understanding and transforming fourth dimensional consciousness in ways that would engender such respect. The question rightly posed by my biographer and his companion and co-worker is, 'What does it truly mean to be human in this context?'

They are working with me. This is a collaborative process.

It should be at least interesting to anyone reading or hearing this so far, that masses of humans are now caught in an imprisoned ignorance of what it means to be human. They still believe they have evolved from apes and have some kind of linear history related to the evolution of your home planet, without any intergalactic or interstellar exchange.

This myopic false understanding leads to a sense of identity that is not only miniscule, but also fundamentally separated from any intimate connection with the living universe of which you are an integral part. An extension of this separated mental bubble is the disconnect with other living beings on your own home planet. It accounts for the almost indescribable violence that human beings inflict upon other species, their own and the animal, vegetable and mineral realms.

In this context, 'equality' would be an inner feeling of respect for the right for all living entities to co-exist, be happy and thrive. Such a feeling and sentiment would alone bring about extremely radical changes in your world, and be a giant step in healing fourth dimensional deformities. In turn, this would usher in a mature evolutionary quantum leap into fifth dimensional consciousness.

Such a shift in fourth dimensional understanding, feeling and sensitivity is one thread of many in a vast tapestry.

Unless humans transform inwardly to a degree that expresses in loving and compassionate behaviour towards all living beings sharing your home planet, the entry into fifth dimensional consciousness will be a reality for the few, and they will eventually have to incarnate on other planets, in other galaxies belonging to your local galactic cluster.

To summarise the thread outlined here: understand equality in the sense of respect and equal right to exist and flourish.

15 Healing

What other threads should you be aware of if you are to heal your fourth dimensional nightmare? The seven Archangels represent seven primary rays, each an archetype representing particular impulses and qualities.

The experiment that is your home planet is specifically related to the question, 'What would happen over time if all seven rays were brought together in one environment?' The symbolic rainbow represents this as an ideal of inter-ray harmony. The potential to evolve such harmony on your home planet does exist, but if that doesn't happen, there is a back-up intention and vision. There always is. No planet, sun or galaxy will exist forever. Whatever is not achieved on your planet will be inherited and passed on, and your own future will have to deal with the consequences.

Multi-dimensional existence is truly matrix-like in ways beyond human comprehension. The mission on your planet for those working towards inter-ray harmony is to heal the wounded threads that have manifested as fourth dimensional disharmony and powerful imbalances in your world society.

The tremendous disturbances that have fed into the incarnational flow of souls must be healed and, to begin with, understood. Without understanding there is no incentive to heal. What most needs to be understood? Why has there been an exponential ever-increasing human population on your planet? It is complex. The word complex keeps coming up, and for good reason.

The physically embodied condition afforded by your planetary home is extremely attractive for souls. Of course it is. Think about it. Sensory experience through physical senses can appear like paradise to non-incarnated souls, and also to those whose incarnational status is far less physical than yours. That this imagined heaven is more like hell for so many is another way of approaching the critical phase of your evolutional process we have been investigating; it is another view of transitioning from third to fifth dimensions.

The influx of souls is a part of the disturbance and needs to be understood. What is often referred to as a biological, procreational instinct actually belongs more to third dimensional impulses than fourth. This is an instinct you share with all other living entities on your planet. The fourth dimension of truly human evolutional life, the various hybrid varieties of that, seven in all, have been strongly influenced by this third dimensional procreational drive. That was as it should be during the long processes of evolutional development on your planet. The planet could sustain the steady increases of humans. It is no accident that during the last few hundred years the increases of the human population have stretched your planetary resources. It is a sign of something out of balance that an exponentially exploding population is happening at a time when it is being understood that you cannot have infinite growth on a finite planet.

There is a deeper situation unfolding here. Humanity is being challenged to shift from a third dimensional driven impulse, that of a procreational influence, towards a fourth dimensional human capacity to redirect and transform this impulse in ways that will truly depart from third dimensional manifestation of purely biological domination. In other words, human potential subsumes the preceding evolutionary dimensions, and advances them towards a truly human vision of what many of your present incarnated souls are naming sustainability.

Can you see how the tension between growth and reduction plays out on your planet, and how the adherents of unlimited growth are like people having many children driven by biological instinct? Therefore this instinct expresses in multiple ways, including the over-influx of souls into reincarnated bodies. It also expresses in every type of over-indulgence that plagues your planet.

16 Experiment

There is another ray stream, related to your galactic evolution, solar system and planet, that is active in other galaxies that are members of your local galactic cluster. The mission unfolding within those galaxies is a variation and extension of what is happening in your home galaxy. This mission has numerous sub-streams. Its over-arching purpose is twofold: to create planetary environments, as with your own home planet, that can accommodate biological and humanoid life as an extension of your own galactic experiment, and secondly to actuate other experiments as variations of primary intentionality and imagery.

I have attended councils that have focused on these galactic-cluster developments, but only as an observer. Sufficient to understand that life in your universe is incredibly diverse, yet related. Souls are essentially universal, and therefore capable of inhabiting any part of your cosmos, potentially. My attachment to your galaxy, solar system and planet is absolutely not arbitrary. The sheer physicality of your incarnational human evolution is unique. It is a unique variation on a primary archetypal theme. What makes it so unique is also what makes it high risk. It isn't the density of the physical and material evolution alone that accounts for its uniqueness. The amazing sophistication of the biological microcosm that humans are, allows for potentials of consciousness, creativity, individuality and future possibilities that outstrip other evolutional streams, but simultaneously, so too are the risks. As souls that have chosen this particular experiment for advanced spiritual motives, there is a type of soul quality that could be described as 'adventurous'. This is not the most stable of cosmic experiments, but neither is it the most predictable. Indeed, the principle of freedom is nowhere as powerful in incarnated status as on your home planet.

This innate quality of various hybrid humans has expressed brilliantly in long lost civilisations that were technologically advanced, and yet not as physically embodied as later humanoids. Each time a planetary civilisation and culture collapses, through rampant out-of-control individualism and indulgence, another deep memory trace is passed on, and the gene pool is strengthened. To the extent that lessons are resisted, they are also weakened through future denser biological embodiments. Resistances are passed on to a greater physicality and vie with the increasingly spiritualised embodiment. This becomes a battle of forces: regressive towards biological impulses and progressive towards spiritualised impulses. The fourth dimension is where human beings embody this battle at its most intense. But this is only a drama within a greater drama that involves the entirety of your galaxy and galactic cluster. Nonetheless it is an important stage even within the context of the whole.

You are truly on the brink of a great splitting. Souls on your planet are separating into different sub-streams with different future consequences beyond what has occurred for millennia. Nothing is as rigid or fixed as words tend to suggest. Hence, when we refer to fourth dimensional, a spectrum is indicated. This spectrum can be expressed as lower, middle and higher fourth dimension. An indication such as this is also a warning to avoid strict demarcations. Humans belong to a shifting spectrum of experience, but the division into three zones can be helpful, even to set one's personal radar appropriately. Lower fourth dimensional relates especially to more automatic, unthinking and biologically-driven consciousness. Middle fourth dimension relates especially to intellectual, questioning and curious consciousness. The higher fourth dimension relates to a metaphysical and spiritually engaged consciousness, but should be distinguished from a truly fifth dimensional state of being. It is yet lacking deep, experiential qualities. An example being someone who reads spiritual books and uses spiritual talk, but without authentic fifth dimensional experience.

Fifth dimensional experience can only be suggested in words, but suffice to say, it goes beyond intellectualism and conceptualism. Words such as compassion, insight, altruism and clarity point in the direction of the fifth dimension, but actions speak louder than words, so fifth dimensional embodiment must include an integrated and holistic trans-human condition: in other words, Homo spiritus.

17 Homo Biotech

There is a cosmic principle, expressing throughout evolutional time and space, relevant to your present planetary situation. This principle is the opposite of unity. It could be named disunity or splitting. When something that has been united splits, it is a significant change. It can also be known as the principle of division. What you refer to as 'one humanity' is splitting. This is so the principle of unity can proceed in new ways.

For millennia, the human experiment on your planet has evolved in two major directions simultaneously. This dual movement has been occurring multi-dimensionally behind the scenes, hidden from ordinary view. Humanity with its ever-increasing number of souls incarnating at any given time has veered towards either the principle of unity or division. When these two directions reach a point of distance from each other, they must separate. This is a cosmic law.

The one species of Homo sapien is splitting into two major subspecies. One will become Homo spiritus and the other Homo biotech. One will evolve into the spiritualised human, the other into a biologically and technologicised human.

These two main sub-streams will no longer be able to inhabit the same environment. As human types they are already diverging to an extreme degree and are for all intents and purposes already splitting, but not yet environmentally. We still share the same environment, breathe the same air.

The splitting is happening inwardly: psychologically, emotionally, mentally and consciously. It is also happening biologically and physiologically. Above all else, the splitting is happening spiritually.

At the same time, those who are evolving in the same general direction are uniting in ways that are more intense and embodied then ever before on your planet.

The dual movement in opposite directions has infiltrated every aspect of your planetary evolutionary culture, everything that human beings can have influence over. A breaking point is eventually reached which must be resolved by either breaking through, breaking down, or both simultaneously.

Splitting and uniting are the 'apocalypse' prophesised by ancient seers. It is inevitable, and belongs to an inner dual impulse manifesting through evolutionary time-space. This dual impulse is within each individual human being and eventually undergoes a splitting. This too splits and allows the impulse to further unite in order to progress.

The cosmic principle therefore plays out microcosmically and macrocosmically as opportunities for greater unity. We can't stop it from happening. But it is possible to evolve into a higher unity.

Homo Biotech is a prime example of the splitting that doesn't achieve a higher unity, and therefore can be perceived as malformed from a higher perspective.

18 Splitting

What happens to the two sub-streams of humanity after they split? Fourth dimensional mentality seeks for a simple understanding, but the evolutional cosmos is profoundly complex. When a major splitting occurs between two incompatible streams a way of understanding this and its consequences cannot be explained simply.

I want to give you a smaller example of splitting that can provide at least some glimpses into what is significant to understand within this complexity. Imagine a marriage between two souls that eventually ends in divorce. From a larger perspective some common features need to be recognised. They are two individuals who came together on the basis of common attractors. They split apart because the attractors were overtaken by divergences and incompatibilities. No matter why they split apart the question I wish to pose is, 'Are they now totally apart?'

Another question could be, 'When they were married were they really totally together?' When two sub-streams of humanity split apart, are they really totally apart? And when one humanity shares one common environment, your planet, are they really totally together?

Remember, you are multi-dimensional beings. Therefore it is vital to grasp how a connection can be at the same time a disconnection, how together and apart can be simultaneous from a complex and multi-dimensional perspective. When I speak of the possibility of Homo sapiens splitting into two differently evolving streams, this does not imply a total separation, but rather an incarnational and environmental separation.

I shall now give you another picture to contemplate. There are seven galaxies in your local cluster. There is at least one solar system with a planet prepared for biological and humanoid life in each of those seven galaxies. Your planet is in one of the seven. These planetary abodes are separate from any other inhabited planets within this galactic cluster. They are specifically created for an expected evolutional event on your home planet. This event has been known about from ancient times and beyond within your planetary history.

The way to approach this seven-planet spectrum is to imagine that human beings have occupied the centre planet, and the three planets on either side represent an evolutional spread of motivational forces.

At one end of the spectrum exists potentially a third dimensional dominated biosphere, whilst at the other end of the spread exists a fifth dimensional dominated biosphere. And where you are in the middle planet in that spread is as a melting pot and sorting house, otherwise known as Homo sapiens.

This is the fourth dimensional experiment and the pull of the entire spectrum of forces are within and without this particular biosphere.

Any splitting into two main evolutional directions is either towards third or fifth dimensional identity and experience. This movement has always happened on your planet, ever since the breeding programs that engendered your human races, but incarnationally within the biospheric environment of your planet.

Whether this can continue in such a fashion is now in the balance. One way or another, a game-changing circuit breaker will happen. Earth time is running out.

19 Consciousness

Having presented a picture that may well appear gloomy, and even depressing, I shall now describe where a portal of light and hope exists within this scenario. Nothing in the unfolding evolution of your solar system experiment is entirely predetermined. There are many examples in your planetary history that demonstrate miraculous changes in circumstances. For instance, the end of the Cold War, coming down of the Berlin Wall, collapse of the Soviet Union, ending of apartheid in South Africa, and many more local, sudden, unexpected changes.

These changes are influenced by trans-dimensional forces, but nonetheless also require changes in human thought and feeling, and most importantly, the will to action. In that sense, they are not predetermined. When a situation reaches a type of stagnated paralysis, something can happen to change it. This is the principle of freedom that especially belongs, as a cosmic blessing, for human beings.

A common expression of third dimensional domination for humanity is what you refer to as consumerism. Consumerism is a force of materialistic addiction. It is a combination of third dimensional biological existence and second dimensional dark matter that provides the foundation for fourth dimensional human capacities to exploit the second and third dimensional kingdoms, by way of advanced imaginations and technical skills.

This becomes a gateway into manufactured production of material objects that, in balance, gives humanity an evolved health, ease and pleasure of embodied life, but when out of balance, can lead to inner blindness that is totally destructive and cancerous.

The consequences of consumerist addiction are too obvious for me to labour the point. And yet for those who are blinded by materialism and physicality, this disease is not so obvious. As this plays out on your planet in overwhelmingly complex and exaggerated ways, it becomes a part of the 'evil empire' that most needs to collapse if a radical shift of your planetary culture is to eventuate, and if a turn-around of your evolution is to occur. Consumerism has contaminated every corner of your global culture. This thread is a dominant force in your planetary coat of many colours.

When fifth dimensional impulses, such as compassion, interconnectedness, respect for all life, altruism, responsibility and authentic caring, to name a few, penetrate into fourth dimensional mental capacity, a rebalancing occurs that shifts consumerism into a humble servant, instead of a tyrannical master.

Materialism and physicality can then become wondrous servants of the Gods, of trans-dimensional intelligences. Then an awakening, embodied soul realises without any doubt that only Supreme energies of the most 'spiritual' nature can satisfy the soul appetites and bring true creativity, understanding, purpose and love of life.

If I can embody again on your planet and bring such messages and ways to transition into fifth dimensional consciousness and living, then I will indeed seek for a suitable portal and geographical location. This depends on a number of unpredictable factors, but it is probable that I will reincarnate before very long. My biography, as with yours, is an ongoing saga. Fascination with any biography is missing the point and usefulness of it being created.

It is common to read many spiritual books without affecting any real change. If my biography is a type of spiritual entertainment, then it is just more materialism. If it's not penetrating deeply into your mind and soul and effecting constructive evolutional change, then it is a waste of energy. At the very least it should be planting seeds that will be watered by life. I knew this during my previous six incarnations. This knowing belongs to a developed sense of mission and purpose.

We are not here to waste our human embodiments. For those many souls who do seemingly waste human incarnations, remember, many are close to awakening and eventually will. Souls inhabiting human embodiments are at vastly different degrees of inner development. You would be amazed if you knew how vast is the spectrum of human beings in terms of their evolutional development. All souls, no matter what type of biological embodiment they inhabit at any given point in time, are passing through experiences that are perfectly understandable from a larger perspective. All souls are developing qualities that eventually will serve the mission and vision of Source and the benevolent Sun beings.

It is the inviolate principle of freedom that allows for deviations from uniformity, and therefore cosmic evolution is absolutely variable and unpredictable in its workings and creative expressions. The saving grace is consciousness: your consciousness, my consciousness and how we inter-relate, communicate and co-create in freedom, joy and love.

PART 3

INNER WORK

20   Deep Listening

A most important evolutionary shift is happening on your planet, despite resistances and obstacles. Uppermost in the manifestations of this shift is the increase in inter-dimensional communications, including this work. Such exchanges have been happening in one form or another, with varying degrees of recognition and understanding, ever since the breeding programs.

In an age like your own, when scientism and atheism reduce human beings to a belief in a separated dimensional existence, communications that are in reality inter-dimensional are often considered as pure imagination, hallucination or insane. This is not to reject actual imaginational, hallucinatory or psychotic states of mind, but even then such experiences are often mixed with actual inter-dimensional communications. This is a very complex phenomenon. And yet the belief in a separated, atheistic dimensionality is actually more hallucinatory than most other positions. Atheists are not necessarily crazy, but sadly misinformed. They may be very spiritual in their essential natures without realising it. They may be more humane than so-called spiritual people. But they also limit their own and others' capacity to engage in inter-dimensional communications. Many of your conservative, non-progressive sciences help to keep this in check. One important way for humans to cultivate the faculty of inter-dimensional communication, not only linguistic, is deep listening.

The evolutional development of individualism especially pronounced among some sub-streams has created an overly strong mental self-identity. The ego, or I, has split off from the collective sense of identity that other sub-streams exhibit. Contrast the European ego with the Indigenous ego in a general way to get a feel for this difference. An overly individuated self-identity can find it difficult to deeply listen to others in embodied encounters. This is a vast topic, but as a general phenomenon it points to a critical area of challenge: that of developing the capacity to receive communications from external sources, especially those that fall outside of one's limited belief system.

A healthy individuality is one that is finely balanced between the poles of individuality and collectivism. The capacity and faculty of deep listening then opens new pathways of experience, including inter-dimensional communications. Fifth dimensional humanity would belong to an inter-dimensional community.

In a real sense, the non-belief in inter-dimensionality is a safeguard, for it keeps those unready for appropriate exchanges at bay. This is to be understood in a non-judgemental way. It is simply important in the evolutional context of your planetary potential, that the faculty of deep listening be cultivated. The biographer has helped in this work, as have many others across your planet, as indeed I did too.

There are many ways to do this important work: in schools, at public events and sacred gatherings, but also in the everyday encounters with each other. It can break down the rigid barriers that overly individuated self identities construct. It is another vital thread in the tapestry of needed evolutional change among those sub-streams that have most developed individualism.

I will further this work of deep listening with increased focus when and if I take my next human embodiment. It is a corrective measure within fourth dimensional evolution.

May we transcend our strong individualities and truly listen to the souls of others. May we deeply connect to other souls with empathy and understanding. May we progress towards the status of Homo spiritus.

21 Interest in Others

A related faculty to deep listening is being interested in others and, by extension, to life. Life can be as a pile of Christmas presents before they are opened. What is in the wrapped packages is a mystery, but will not be so forever. At the appointed hour the outer wrappings will be removed and all will be revealed.

Many humans no longer believe in mysteries. For them it is as if Christmas presents don't exist. Or they already think they know what's under the wrappings ,so there is nothing to discover.

This analogy can be applied to how many humans perceive others, themselves and the universe. They have no deep interest in anything. Life is humdrum and mundane. When this becomes a chronic condition, even suicide can feel preferable to living.

Being interested in others suggests a depth of feeling, sincerity and consciousness free of ulterior motives. Such interest, though, must also include oneself.

Why should you be interested?

I will tell you. In truth you are mysterious beings with qualities and multi-dimensional aspects that await discovery. You are more than you seem and more than you can ever know. You are like an eternal pile of unopened Christmas gifts always awaiting revelation at the appointed hour, and so is everyone else and everything else.

This understanding offers a bridge for you to venture across. On the other side you will rediscover the childlike quality of wonder.

This quality is fourth dimensional but when matured to include all living beings and the living cosmos becomes an initiation into fifth dimensional inter-being and inter-communication.

This must start where you are and turned inside-out and outside–in. It is why you must seek teachers, books, art and any other internal practice or external aid that helps to motivate your interest in life.

22 Meditation

Meditation, rightly understood, is an antidote to the intrusions of the saboteur. The saboteur is known as the Asuras in your Eastern symbology. In your Western symbology they are known as demons or devils.

These adversaries are also inter-dimensional and now have access to human minds and emotions in ever more subtle ways.

Meditation needs to be understood in new contexts in your present environment. Your environment has radically changed since I was last incarnated in the early twentieth century.

Technology has developed at an astonishing rate, and yet consciousness will always be superior to even the most advanced technology. Meditation and consciousness must be understood together.

The only way to overcome the biotechnical saboteur, and bring it into subservience to consciousness, is to neutralise it.

The saboteur has been a part of your universe from the very beginning of second dimensional life.

The symbol of God's favourite angel, Lucifer, a being of dazzling light falling from grace, indicates what type of force we are dealing with here. Lucifer represents the principle of freedom, but there is a price to pay. Freedom implies consciousness that can separate from Source to the degree that wilful imagination can function. Meditation is a way to bring Lucifer back into line, and only then can he behave in alignment with Source, as a servant of Source.

Lucifer has armies of his own serving his desires rather than those of Source. These are the Asuras. They serve individualism and the freedom to act on behalf of personal desires. Meditation is a way of killing the Asuras. They will always return, but every time they are slain,

Source enjoys emptiness and can create anew with all the original graces of wisdom, love, peace and universal impulses directed towards fifth dimensional spiritualised embodiment.

Every time the adversaries return, meditation and practices, rightly understood, can kill them, and they can be transformed gradually into servants of Source. This is their destiny, and when they are fully transformed they will not have to be slain again.

Contemplate this deeply, and practice a way of meditation that is a portal into emptiness and full consciousness of primary Beingness.

So be it!

23 Openness

The cracks in the wall of a mind imprisoned in hopelessness and despair must bring questioning that opens new possibilities. Without this questioning the darkened walls of depression and futility can overwhelm the soul.

It is a primary part of our intentional mission and soul-inspired impulse to experiment with ways to help those lost sheep to question their resigned and hopeless mental prisons. Deep listening can help, but also being alert to windows of opportunity to say the right thing at the right time.

Behind the veil of despair and hopelessness there is always a question. This question can be the first glimmer of light in the darkness, but it needs to be articulated, as a hook that pulls the questioner into a field of possibilities. Good questions can lead to other questions. It is a long way from believing in nothing to accepting the fact that one is an interstellar being, but many have journeyed across the abyss and survived to tell the story. The belief that nothing makes sense and there is no higher purpose can be met with deep empathy, and at the right moment a gentle alternative view can be expressed.

This biography is not going to help those whose rejection of such contents is fixed and strong. As light bearers we can only offer a helping hand to those who freely agree to receive. Ultimately it's a matter of time before every soul is ready to take a step that will lead towards light.

On your planet, materialism and physicality provide temptations so powerfully alluring, yet offering no lasting peace and satisfaction, so that eventually questions must emerge. Is this it? What now? Why am I still discontent, even though I have everything that material and physical sensory experience can offer? What is missing? Is there someone who can point the way out of this black hole? Is there a way out?

The questions will be uniquely personal and archetypally universal. It will be the beginning of a way to salvation, if followed correctly. If it isn't dismissed, but a little genuine openness, a crack in the dark wall of hopeless despair occurs, the road becomes a way that promises 'something' and can be followed.

This is part of fourth dimensional service. Never give up on anyone. This too I tried to address in various ways during my previous incarnation. It is the essential tone of therapeutic practice underlying external methods. It is genuine compassion in action.

Of course not all souls are drowning in such pits of dark despair, but remember there are two main orientations. Every step in the right direction is a step away from the wrong direction. We are all in this together, incarnate, discarnate and transcarnate souls who belong to the rays of service.

Remain close to those who are strong in their understanding and actions, those who walk their talk, and those who you can cooperatively work with towards fourth dimensional healing and fifth dimensional awakening.

24 Alignment

What is desire and where does it come from? Source did desire. It desired to create a universe to experiment with and in, but when rays were permitted to have freedom to create in their manners, desire too became variegated. Desire therefore in its purest essence emanates from Source, and when human desire aligns with Source, it is a force for good, harmony, unity and peace.

When desire becomes separated from Source and aligned with other impulses, it leads to various forms of suffering and dissatisfaction. Buried deep down in all human souls is the desire for alignment with Source. It is this desire that expresses as an impulse towards spiritual experience and understanding.

Desire should not be cast out as an enemy of healthy fourth dimensional consciousness, nor fifth dimensional spirituality, but harnessed to Source, like a wagon to horses. Desire in this context is close in meaning to passion. Source is passionate about evolutional unfoldment towards spiritualised embodiment.

Without desire, human souls are without enthusiasm. In ancient Greece 'enthusiamus' was considered a vital component of a spiritually enlivened person. The dull, inert, semi-depressed norm of your present industrialised societies is mostly because materialistic and physical sensory overload has robbed souls of deep desire and passion. It is vital, as part of fourth dimensional healing, that individuals ask questions of themselves and each other such as, "What do you love doing?", and then actually doing it.

This is the open secret of my biographical journey through many incarnations, and believe me, when a soul follows this path of discovering and acting on deep desire and passion aligned with Source, one begins to understand the mission and purpose of one's life, even beyond any particular incarnation.

What does it mean to be aligned with Source as a human being living in the twenty-first century? During my biographer's present incarnation alone there has been exponential growth in all sectors of your global society.

Exponential is a word that needs deep understanding. It means that the rate of growth is increasing constantly. This creates problems on all levels and in all facets of your planetary existence. It polarises the positives and negatives in an ongoing process towards critical tipping points. It is also a double-edged sword, providing opportunities to align with Source unprecedented in recent human history, or possibilities of catastrophic consequences.

Humanity is on an evolutionary knife edge. If one can become aware of the increased temptations that exponential growth brings about, it is possible to cultivate inner defences and antidotes. This should be blatantly obvious is the areas of technology and materialism.

The new war on your planet is largely an economic one. Economics has become the fundamental topic of your global civilisation. Economic policy is how your elite controls directions of exponential growth. This is complex and many are describing the mechanics of how this operates to enslave your population. But interestingly this enslavement is with the approval of many of the enslaved, because the allurements and temptations of consumerism and technology are so powerful that only a genuine spiritual consciousness can overcome them.

If human beings overcame the addiction to materialism, technology and sensory desire, these aspects of your planetary evolution could be useful secondary servants of a sane, wise and compassionate humanity. Economics could serve all your planetary advancement in ways that lead to the emergence of Homo spiritus.

Exponential growth in itself is a mighty problem. You cannot endure continued exponential growth on a finite planet. To turn this around, or even stabilize growth will require a quantum shift in consciousness brought about by voluntary means, or by a response to catastrophe, and it may then be too late to recover from the latter on your present home planet.

To align with Source in your present era will require mass refusal to feed the monster of materialistic over-production, with its commercial advertising empires. It will also require new rebellious forms of education, and more than anything else it will require a shift in consciousness within individual souls.

The effects of exponential growth on the fragile garden planet you call home are already dire. It will take more than my words to change this, but everyone can make a difference.

Multitudes of drips can become a stream. Many streams joining can become a river, and rivers can find their ways to an ocean. You need oceanic change, but don't neglect the drops.

25 Honesty

Merging my consciousness and subtle energy with my biographer's as he sits in a cafe is a fresh experiment, a significant one as he informs me he will be travelling for the next few days. It is in the midst of everyday world circumstances that fourth dimensional consciousness must be transformed and healed. I was present with him last night during a powerful group encounter, which followed a series of important meetings with souls who are a vital part of his working cluster. To use a cliché, 'the net widens.'

It is time to give a spiritual name to my biographer. It has already been chosen but has been in abeyance for some years. If I have been named so should he. His name can be Vayu. Elucia and Vayu in this particular setting can therefore be a real-time experiment in your fourth-dimensional world. Details become more significant as we proceed. The theme of last night's group gathering was trauma and how to heal it, an important topic in relation to many of my previous communications. For instance, the saboteur that especially hones in on weaknesses caused by trauma. Every soul carries the traumas of history as well as more personal and recent traumas. These traumas vary immensely in strength and conscious recognition. Acknowledging these layers of trauma is an important step in transforming their energy into soul gifts.

Sometimes an event happens that triggers the trauma. You are all potential trauma survivors. You are all potential transformers and transcendentalists. Imagine sitting in a public place with many people passing by. Who are they? Who are you? Why do you exist in this fourth dimensional reality? Are we not all attempting to transform weakness into strength, trauma into creative possibilities?

The ways of woundedness are many. Some are obvious, but many are subtle and hidden from ordinary view. Humans have become masters of disguise. Until you individually and collectively begin to be honest, the wounds of unhealed traumas will persist, even if below ordinary consciousness.

Your present collective condition has become so fractured that you no longer understand the words you speak. This is especially true of honesty. As Native Americans realised about Europeans who raped their people and land, 'they speak with forked tongues.'

I told you about economic control, now I will tell you of another aspect of your present enslavement. It is the age of lies. You have been lied to since babyhood. Your entire culture has lied to you in myriads of ways. Lying has been perpetrated by third dimensional biological drives aided by fourth dimensional intellectual cleverness, driven by a massive abuse of freedom and a stunning lack of discipline. Very few humans on your planet remain unscathed by this exponential spread of intricate webs of lies. The way you then develop includes layers of dishonesty that largely become unconscious.

When a particular inner characteristic becomes a cultural norm, few perceive it for what it is. The ways of dishonesty are so embedded in your global cultures by this time, that most hardly notice.

A greater problem is how this plays out within individuals, because that is where it needs to be transformed. Fourth dimensional healing must therefore include radical honesty. This must begin with oneself. What really motivates you to be the way you are? How would it be if you communicated and acted with deep honesty?

All of my incarnational and discarnational communications are founded on honesty. If I err it is never because I lie. I give you this teaching as a powerful tool in your journeys towards fourth dimensional balance and fifth dimensional awakening.

Do not deceive yourselves and you will become greater advocates of honesty and transformation. Begin to model what you understand, no matter the price you have to pay. Stop going along with mutual and collective modes of deception, dishonesty and ulterior motives.

Move gradually towards a purity of soul and spiritual embodiment that is worthy of your greatest and noblest insights.

Begin by meditating and contemplating the ways your dishonesty conceals your wounds. Your wounds offer gateways into transformed being and living.

Be truly human. Do not escape from the mission you are intimately aligned with in the depths of your souls.

Burn in the fires of deep honesty and a miracle of existential change will occur.

I promise you this.

26 Compassion

Trauma is a natural part of inter-dimensional evolution. It has metabolised within third and fourth dimensional biological and human incarnations, and it is within fourth dimensional human embodiment that trauma must be transfigured and transformed.

Understand the roots of trauma. Trauma is when something leaves a painful inter-dimensional memory, often below the threshold of consciousness. Trauma is experience not fully accepted. It resides in resistance to life's unpleasant experiences. It is personal in its relativity: what is traumatic to one person may not be so to another. Therefore, the roots of trauma are within the person, not in the event itself. The resolution too is within the person.

Trauma occurs on many levels and is inter-generational. Fourth dimensional healing needs to take this into account. The most universal level of trauma belongs to the experiences that all biological life has had, and continues to encounter. This is where trauma and empathy interweave. You suffer for others, and that can include other biological life beyond our own species. This is the deepest level of trauma, and is natural. But in order to heal this type of universal trauma you must understand and accept that by transitioning into biological incarnation Source became truly physical, and physical beings undergo what humans refer to as pain, or if intense, trauma. Humanity has inherited that from their distant past.

Where trauma can be transformed into compassion is when, through empathy, fifth dimensional qualities arise. For instance, if humans empathised with the suffering animals pass through, they would immediately stop abusing them as they do. They would honour nature in the same way. There would also be no more wars or genocides. The more human oriented level of trauma belongs to your own species. Then there is the level of your own group identity, your family, and finally yourself.

Your personal trauma has its roots in personal identity, and it is exactly here that change can occur. You are more than you, and more than your trauma. Who you think you are is so limiting, it holds personal trauma in a gridlock. It freezes trauma in self-oriented identity.

Personal biography over-identified with one's present incarnation, or even many incarnations, holds trauma in a memory bank. The way to release this energy is by gradually realizing who you really are in all its mystery. Then you can break free of the story that you are held in.

27 A Strong Heart

The addictions adopted through embodied space-time are escapisms from the energy of trauma. It is these addictions that feed your industrial and technological age. If you are addicted to teddy bears, someone will produce them for you in abundance, and try to convince you that life is not worth living without a never ending supply of varieties of teddy bears. Fourth dimensional narcissism is a parasite that lives off the various types of trauma escapisms.

The greatest traumas are hopelessness and purposelessness, and there are many addictive sweeteners to cover over this existential black hole. Only authentic spiritual experience and understanding can cure addictions that are rooted in existential trauma.

This is the cutting edge of my biography, the darkness I would urge you to explore and pass through, into the light.

Here is where true salvation awaits. Is there more for me to communicate?

Embodied human life will always provide multiple challenges. Vayu can acknowledge this. Reality always puts theory into the shade. Trusting in the grace of spirit doesn't give cheap prizes, and this often becomes a solo challenge.

Life is what happens while you are planning something else. It isn't always a straight road with easy to read sign posts, and the only principle that is truly predictable is unpredictability. There is never a real adventure without unexpected situations. Welcome to fourth dimensional human incarnational existence!

It was never any different for me. It takes a strong heart. You are so bamboozled by material and physical phenomena surrounding you, it is easy to forget that you are embodied spirit.

I am aware of Vayu's challenges. In the midst of the challenges, he gives thanks to spirit. This is as it should be. It is the great testing ground of embodied spirit, with its joys and sorrows.

Follow your heart, and take the plunge. Discover how to contribute to the great work.

PART 4

THE GREAT WORK

28 The Implicate Order

It has been called the implicate order by one of your physicists. It is order behind chaos. It is Creator's intention, observable as cosmic order in countless galaxies, all co-existing. Your universe is not at war with itself. Even the relatively tiny solar system that your planet is an even more minuscule part of, is exemplifying an implicate order.

A healthy biological or human body is another even tinier example, and so on into realms of atoms and molecules that follow the same cosmic principle. This is the model your mind and societies should be following. Spiritual consciousness obeys the implicate order.

Fourth dimensional consciousness must reflect this in its intellectual and creative endeavours if humankind is to not be at odds with the universe.

If you were to retranslate the language of the implicate order into humanly inspired emotional communications, you may emerge with poetry of the most compelling beauty and wisdom. The music and harmony of the spheres could be another way of describing the implicate order.

For you spiritual warriors fighting off the demons of inertia and mental blindness, the implicate order provides a reminder and encouragement to create a planetary culture truly worthy of future Homo spiritus. You are pioneers and torch-bearers.

You must walk among the living dead and bring them life. You must work with me and my loving hosts, and open windows where air has putrefied. I am here helping every step of the way, but in freedom you must overcome all that will block your path.

Behind variations in external manifestations that seem to defy strict order, there is a super order. This super order is as inviolate a principle as freedom. It operates even when all else breaks down. It is the creative force of the universe, and your soul nature. Your planetary biosphere with its amazing varieties of species, co-exists in ways that are self-regulating, and reveal for those with the eyes to see, a harmony that is beautiful, glorious and intelligent. You must do what you can to awaken yourselves, and by virtue of your own reborn senses, others.

Entire generations of newly incarnated souls are being bombarded by technology, and enslaved in increasingly sophisticated forms of manufactured escapisms. Your divided human sub-streams have become the ground where the battle now takes place. The awakening ones walk among the living dead who see them not.

I will come and create a virtual storm. You must prepare the way. The storm must come and wash away the filth.

Your garden planet is far too precious to simply stand by and observe its demise. Do not be timid. That does not mean becoming rude or arrogant, but timidity only helps feed the beast.

Speak truth with unashamed dexterity and skill. Be flexible while passing through rigidity. Be open when in enclosed spaces. Be bold when among those cowering in fear. Speak truth to those whose eyes and ears are closed, if there be an opening for light to enter.

Express your soul vision to those who can be of help. Do the great work in ways that sacrifice all that is not vital.

Do not waste energy on trivialities. Indeed, rest, knowing that your revitalization is also a service to the great work. This is the hour of God. One of our cluster said so not long ago.

Never lose heart, because there is more happening that you can ever know.

29 Soul Clusters

What is a soul cluster? Over vast evolutionary time, relationships develop between souls who are attracted to each other because of mutual interests or concerns. It is an illusion to believe that relationships that have bonding qualities are discontinued when souls separate, including when we pass through the gate of death. This is simply not the case.

All souls belong to a network of other, caring souls that exist transcarnationally, in other words, incarnationally and discarnationally. It is a fundamental truth that no soul is truly alone. No soul is unloved or uncared for. Furthermore, the potential to engage with our soul family, so to speak, that group of caring souls that we belong to, offers opportunities to redirect our focus, energies, and activities in evolutionarily constructive ways. 'Soul cluster' does not imply a rigid group of souls exclusively separated from others. Soul cluster is a fluid, open-ended dynamic of relationships, that have as their innermost reality, what you refer to as love, caring, empathy, companionship and mutual creativity. Just as an incarnated soul may make a new, special friend at any moment, no-one is excluded from becoming a part of, or being accepted into one's own soul cluster. There are no rigid demarcations.

But having said that, the relationships that have been forged over evolutionary time and space, that have the deepest resonances between souls, are those that offer the greatest opportunities for those experiences that we can refer to as fifth dimensional or spiritual. Those experiences transcend the individual ego, and belong to a sublime, profound sense of belonging to something greater than oneself, where the soul's deepest yearnings can be realised and satisfied. For we all belong to the living company of souls that inhabit your universe.

What might happen if a group of us who belong to the same soul cluster, and have developed relationships over numerous incarnations, were to reincarnate at the same time? Even those who previously incarnated at separate times might now realise it is time to join forces in your physical environment, in ways that allow close working proximity to naturally occur. This is an unprecedented process being debated discarnationally at this time. You are invited to also discuss this and contribute.

If the train doesn't get to its destination one way, it will another. Does it matter by which route? Yes and no. From an ultimate destination point of view, it doesn't matter, but it does matter because Source is real and Source matters. Therefore, everything matters. We exist in a dynamic universe. As such, there is no ultimate destination.

Remember the event horizon? It works forwards as well as backwards. How then does the route matter? We need an analogy. Someone has an inspired vision. Let us imagine it is to create a particular creative project. Does it matter how this person proceeds? Of course it does. Some ways will never succeed and others will. Some will succeed better than others. This is not random or arbitrary. If Source has a vision, then the route matters.

The intentions underlying one's deepest desires are filtering through as signatures of one's destiny. This develops into very refined qualities that are soul gifts that interweave into the evolving culture. This matters greatly. Culture is the collective outcome of all the incremental choices that individual souls make. My biographer is developing soul qualities of networking and inter-dimensional biographical communication.

My biography is vaster and more complex than I could write when incarnated. It is also more interwoven with those of my soul cluster than has been obvious until now. This is the era of incarnated soul cluster work.

As above so below.

30 Planetary Shifts

When soul cluster work begins to shift your planetary culture into new necessary directions, it will become obvious in ways that are not happening now. These shifts need to happen. What will they look like?

When the storms come, so will the shifts. Behind the extreme storms, will be the signs of the implicate order. Few will realise the reality of what is happening. It cannot be otherwise.

The storms will be powerful enough to instigate a collapse of existing structures. People will be so numbed by fourth dimensional addictive comas, that at first they will behave as if nothing unusual is occurring. They will even enjoy the storms as more fourth dimensional entertainment.

But a point will be reached when even the most desensitised will begin to awaken to the fact that something unusually powerful is happening. Economic constructs will not be able to cope. The banking system will collapse. Infrastructure will undergo massive deconstruction.

If this is happening in your lifetime, please welcome this with open eyes and spiritual faith. You will find yourselves in the right places at the right times. There are no accidents.

Witness the shifts with wonder and hope. What you refer to as climate change is simply a consequence of fourth dimensional neurosis and aeons of fractured consciousness. If these storms do not illicit some fear than it is not the real time of reckoning.

All these changes are merely the opening stanza of a wondrous transformation. You will know it without any doubt. It is when, following wave after wave of storm, the beginnings of a new openness will occur.

Eventually many of those who hold the reigns of power will be deposed. They will have no answers. This will herald in a new consciousness. Much of what the masses thought to be important will no longer be so. Technological systems will malfunction. People will have to look each other in the eye and talk to each other. Those who are capable of inner change, will.

In the meantime, take whatever steps bring you closer to the new and the collapse of the old. Understand how ingrained old patterns are, and make extra efforts to be more conscious of them. Develop more discipline to combat those habits that do not serve the higher purpose and mission. Be humbled by your weaknesses. They are gateways into evolutionary growth.

Cultivating fourth dimensional skill is an awesomely challenging task. Helping others transform destructive energies into constructive avenues of creative living requires much wisdom and compassion, that can only be garnered by lifetimes of earnest endeavour.

The words 'universal' and 'university' are linked. True learning has universality and unity as motivating forces. Education must educate the whole person.

It is difficult to reincarnate into a twenty-first century embodiment and not be swept into materialistic and technological glamour, and the sheer power of its influences. And yet these evolving manifestations of fourth dimensional ingenuity offer opportunities to become more universal and cosmopolitan. As with all expressions of human creativity, they can be used in the service of dark forces or of light.

The problem does not reside within materialism and technology, rather in the human agency. It is not the weapon that holds the power but the weapon's owner. When fifth dimensional qualities transform wayward fourth dimensional behaviour, a constructive use of materialism and technology can emerge. This is when humans become rulers of machines.

This would translate into radically changed streams of individual and collective action. The entire global network of consumerism would transition into a zero growth sustainable society. Every aspect of global culture would shift to a more honest, ethical and sane civilization.

Politics, education, media, economy, production, technology and health would all undergo massive transformational change. In one sense your world needs a circuit breaker from any one of those main arteries that co-govern humanity. The virus of fourth dimensional power-lust and rabid narcissism has taken over your civilization. It rules absolutely, and humanity for the most part is firmly enslaved.

It is therefore of paramount importance that circuit breakers occur within the main branches of your societal structures. It doesn't matter what branch, because a real shift in any one branch would have potent consequences in all others.

The dire necessity for transformational shifts belongs with the interface between individuals and society, where every action becomes significant.

Spirituality must become more humanised. It must speak in relevant fourth dimensional language. It must integrate the best of science. It must use technology to inform in ways that reach out to the masses. It must inspire individuals to participate in social reform.

31 Fifth Dimensionality

Fourth dimensional reality includes the human body. This means that fifth dimensional spirituality resides in a physically finite embodiment. Therefore, it is important to preserve the health of this biological organism as much as possible. This is easier said than done, but a mighty incentive is omnipresent.

Spiritual agencies can only effectively use healthy human embodiments. As fifth dimensional energies influx into fourth dimensional human embodiments, a subtle shift occurs. The fourth and third dimensional sheaths become lightened. The actual molecules undergo transmutation. Molecular density becomes more spacious.

This alchemical transfiguration is experienced as a discernable shift in mental, emotional and physiological sensations. You become enlightened in sensory lightened ways. This is the realm of fifth dimensional occupancy. A sixth dimension would become substantially free of attachment to fourth dimensional human embodiment.

This picture allows a glimpse into the greater epic of your universe's evolution. Anything that does not further this evolutionary progression falls back like humus into previous dimensional existence, where it undergoes refinement and becomes part of future re-growth. Ultimately, nothing is wasted. But the most dynamic and living forces are those that are progressively evolutional in character.

You have advanced far, and as human beings are on a most significant threshold. You can move ahead into fifth dimensional spiritualised embodiment, or fall back into third dimensional biologically driven embodiment. The melting pot where these two forces meet is the fourth dimensional human incarnation.

Your discarnate soul cluster and affiliated transcarnate inter-dimensional councils are now increasing energy down-flows into all incarnate humans that are sufficiently receptive. Many are acknowledging this, but others are being shifted subconsciously.

As this occurs, the forces of resistance will attempt to forestall change, and this will play out as it will.

To assist in this evolutional drama, do what you can to stay healthy in body and mind. Others and I are preparing to enter the fray as newly incarnated beings, to further progress this epoch-changing situation.

Blessings!

32 Restoration

The reality underlying human incarnation is far more complex than even most spiritual scientists can grasp. Decisions to incarnate as human beings are limited by particular factors. These factors change within evolutional time.

Individuated souls incarnate into third dimensional planetary life as multitudes of different species. As non-human species become extinct or endangered, they must find other types of embodiments. This is allowed. Therefore, what happens to all biological creatures on your planet affects overall reincarnational processes.

When it comes to human incarnations there has been an unnatural imbalance, influenced by how biological entities are treated. An analogy is a school system and university where all the students are mixed together in ways that are incompatible: kindergarten youngsters in classes with high school students, primary school students with university graduates and so on. When incarnations become mixed in this way, humanity as a whole becomes dramatically unstable. This syndrome has been occurring since the onset of the breeding programs, but the degree to which this has upset your planetary balance has altered.

There is a metamorphic cycle involved, but I wish to explain some peculiar features that are presently occurring on your planet.

Third dimensional biological drives were meant to be humanised by fourth dimensional intellect, but particular ray-strains belonging to primary ray-intentions became so prevalent and dominant, great imbalances became culturally embedded. Many souls incarnating into human embodiments are poorly equipped to deal with such circumstances. The energy resonances that exist between discarnate souls and incarnated potential parents have become chaotic from a higher spiritual perspective.

Highly evolved souls often have to take on very unsuitable parents and families, in order to continue their planetary missions. This is partly because of the vast increase of souls desiring human embodiment. Although this is helping to shift third dimensional entities and qualities into fourth dimensional incarnation, it is in reality inter-dimensional unsustainability. Paradoxically, this will change as human incarnations become less desirable. Another factor is a vast diminishing of fertility rates due to biological and chemical effects. This will happen before too long, if the necessary changes in many related areas do not take place on your planet.

Order will be restored. This is a universal default position. It is the message that resounds through your universe. You have a say in how this will take place. A

heartbreaking spectacle within your present fourth dimensional planetary situation is the many souls who have great potential, and yet are withering away in depression and feelings of purposelessness. This is an ugly by-product of the dominant powers that have infiltrated all sectors of your global societies.

The obvious manifestations appear so overwhelming and unchangeable that it renders many souls into deep, dark and desperate inner landscapes, so bleak that some opt out altogether. Your present societies, and especially the more industrialised and affluent ones, have become pawns to materialism in the shape of capitalistic corporate driven enterprises.

The flow down effect into media, politics, business, advertising, technology, education, law, health, and every other aspect of life is so glaringly omnipresent for all but a few, that for souls whose inner constitutions have developed fifth dimensional sensitivities, it can be experienced as a nightmarish prison or hell. The saving graces are all around, but for souls who are lost in this evil quagmire, created by darkest motives of power-lust and narcissism, it can seem hopeless both personally and collectively.

The bigger picture that my biography is hopefully articulating and depicting, is one of many that humanity needs at this time, yet there are no easy solutions or fixes for those who are as lost sheep. My message is for you light-bearers to not give up on anyone. Every word and action that leans towards and emanates from natural elements of deepest human nature are as drops of stellar nectar, and counter the forces of darkness.

At the same time, it behoves every incarnated soul to transform the darker forces within into streams of service to the great vision of Source. The supreme vision aligns with the deepest visions you are personally capable of achieving.

If a message, word or action from you doesn't reach a lost soul, do not despair. Another light-bearer may be the hundredth monkey. The same vice versa.

You may be planting a seed that will burst into sunlight at a later moment in evolutionary time. Every thought and action can veer towards balance, and integrate what otherwise would be disparate, conflicting or isolating elements.

You are individually part of a soul team greater and more powerful than you can ever imagine.

33 Transcendence

It is important to comprehend what transcendence is. Transcendence is the capacity to experience beyond a particular paradigm or dimension. This is the gateway to interdimensional awareness, and what fourth dimensional maturity inevitably brings a sincere soul to.

How to transcend is a vital part of what authentic spiritual practices cultivate. The conscious choice to sacrifice an attachment that blocks transcendence is an entry point to another dimension.

This must be understood intelligently, within appropriate contexts, as with all deeper topics.

Any method or practice that allows for a true transcendental experience is an intimate friend on the transitional journey from fourth to fifth dimensional embodiment. It is also a preparation for passing over the threshold of death.

Human embodiment is a life university like no other. It offers the promise of a five dimensional integrated embodiment, because each dimension subsumes those that precede it.

The demonic obstruction is a part of freedom that allows for overcoming. Without overcoming, there would be no conscious joy or bliss. Indeed, without contrast, comparison and discernment, there would be no universe like your own.

Freedom implies Lucifer, and permits the free indulgence of sensory desire that becomes all the stronger when embodied. That is why Lucifer was God's favourite angel, metaphorically speaking, because God desired too. But Lucifer must ultimately be re-united with Source, with God's desire. This too is your microcosmic mission. Transcendence is one most significant way for Lucifer to be humbled and transformed.

I will storm the gates of Lucifer's abode of sensual desire with compassion, love and wisdom. Be at peace. This is all a part of a cosmic drama that is bigger than your traumas.

Blessings.

34 The Great Overcoming

Now we arrive at a universal blind spot that must be brought into the light of consciousness. There is an existential anxiety that belongs to a fact that is difficult to accept, no less to understand.

What human beings sense as an essential weakness in their innermost natures is actually shared by and primarily belongs to Source. In mythic terms, God allowed Lucifer, his most beloved of angels, to fall from grace. This implies, and correctly so, that God, the supreme metaphor, is responsible for all the consequences that followed Lucifer's demise. It means that God shares in our human, all too human, struggle.

There is no separation between Source and the evolutional struggle that expresses, for instance, in every fourth dimensional disturbance and wayward disharmony. This brings a question into clear focus. Why did Source allow this to happen?

In understanding this you can transform existential guilt, shame and confusion into liberated consciousness and creative, peaceful, deep understanding.

Without Source sacrificing a part of itself in freedom, you would exist in a clockwork universe. Lucifer was the most beloved angel because he was free to think, desire and create independently of his parent. This is replicated microcosmically, for example when a human child breaks free of parental control and exercises independence.

What is vital to comprehend is that your guilt, fear and shame, our very innermost struggles to mature independently, belong not simply to the human condition, but also to Source itself. If you blame yourselves for your inherent human weaknesses, then think again. You must blame God too, but only as a step towards passing beyond blame altogether.

In forgiving self and God, you can pass beyond forgiveness altogether. You will then enter the hallowed hall of deepest understanding. There is a price to pay for freedom, but the rewards are second to none.

This points to the 'Great Overcoming'. You as representatives of Source will overcome the very obstacle that you have instigated in the first place. You will overcome yourselves. Source will overcome itself through its own creation.

Unity will then be restored, not in its original singularity, but in manifestation and relationship. Fifth dimensional homeostasis is the reward for completing this evolutionary mission.

If you like, this can be viewed as the master game underlying all other games within your universe.

The essential message contains the healing of the split between your human guilt, shame and anxiety and that belonging to Source. Bring them into alignment, and the struggle becomes shared, and so does the overcoming.

Blessings.

35 A New Language

When using words like God, Satan and Lucifer, it is of paramount importance to understand metaphor and symbolism. From early in the development of human language there was a creative challenge between inner experience and outer expression. Early cave art and then hieroglyphics were visual ways of expressing that were capable of common understanding.

As human beings evolved from the hybrid breeding programs, there followed exponential expansions of consciousness and sophisticated capacities to express. The organs of speech developed to allow for intellectual and imaginative abilities way beyond cave wall drawings, and was augmented by writing that far superceded hieroglyphics.

This allowed for new forms of self-expression. Such developments belong to rays that needed to incorporate written language as against those that didn't. These new forms of linguistic self-expression allowed for two quite diverse streams of utilisation, one practical and the other psychological: psychological in an essential sense of capacities translating and transmitting inner experience into comprehensible and coherent messages. Messages are, after all, means by which humans communicate to each other, beyond mere technical information, such as what plants are good to eat.

Messages then become abstract, in other words, communicating subtle nuances of meaning, an example being stories that impart moral injunctions. Indeed, storytelling was an early form of communication that superseded information sharing. This is the foundation of your creative use of metaphor. You must penetrate into a deep sense of what metaphor is. A metaphor is more than a metaphor, pointing beyond itself to truths that cannot be easily expressed directly in ordinary language. Metaphors used by fifth dimensional consciousness transmit spiritual principles or gnosis, knowledge, into relatable symbolic language.

When fourth dimensional mental ability overly literalises metaphor, it stops being metaphor. Its life is deadened. It becomes a rigid and limited photograph, replacing a dynamic, living force. For example, God and Lucifer are metaphors. They are linguistic inventions, creative metaphors pointing beyond themselves, to that which by nature exists in a nameless and trans-metaphoric space. God is Source, and Lucifer is an aspect of Source defined by the word 'freedom.'

You must meditate and contemplate deeply to grasp the essence of these metaphors as inner revelation and liberated consciousness.

This becomes an interweaving of fourth and fifth dimensional consciousness, the transition into Homo spiritus.

36 Reconciliation

One sign that the necessary shift is happening on your planet will be a movement towards understanding and implementing inclusiveness in all areas of human activity. This especially includes how individuals regard themselves. Allow me to explain.

The segregation and separation of tendencies within the psyche of a human being becomes transposed onto the external world. What is not integrated within becomes separated without. If all the elements existing within the individual were to be envisaged as separate entities, then all these entities are required to meet together in a great hall of reconciliation. They all need to express and be heard. Consciousness itself, in its primary neutral and trans-karmic purity needs to adjudicate.

This becomes the model for inner and outer processes of reconciliation. In time, this model heals and allows for enemies to become friends, who can work together in ways that would have been impossible before reconciliation. Whether this 'movement' begins externally or internally, it must by necessity include both if your planetary evolution is to continue without dire consequences. Your present global tendencies to segregate and categorise individuals, nations, creeds and everything that can be distinguished as separate has created a chaotic melting pot of inequality, prejudice, scapegoating and conflict, together with all manner of emotional and psychological disturbances, that spill out into genocide, war and every type of inhumane, narcissistic action imaginable.

You have inherited this tendency from the very first separation from Source, because where there is separation, there is potential for conflict. Nonetheless, in freedom the particular ray streams have evolved with the inclusion of countless choices that have consequences, and this is one way of understanding karma in its greater universal context.

As true as this is, your human condition is at the evolutionary cutting edge of a complex ongoing process. You cannot blame the past, or Source, or anything else if you desire to contribute to positive future change. You as a soul have always been a part of the history of your universe. As interstellar and intergalactic citizens we are all co-participants in this unfolding story. No one can be excluded in processes of reconciliation. If you are able, begin with reconciling all the disparate elements within yourselves. You must stop the inner war.

37 Transformation

It would appear that another wave of violence has happened on your home planet. Do you think there is anything new about this? Are you interested in a fifth dimensional perspective concerning human violence? Firstly, you must gain insight into the deepest meaning of freedom. In your myth of Lucifer falling from grace, you have the greatest clue. Please understand that the names given in this transmission are your inventions. Names are only surface descriptions for innumerable forces and powers existing in your planetary life. With this in mind, I will explain something that relates to your present planetary circumstances.

Lucifer separated from Source only with permission from Source. Lucifer was the favourite Archangel of Source because he was closest to Source in every way, and that especially included freedom. The freedom of Source is omnipotent, but Lucifer only approximates that. Human beings are in the same position as Lucifer, except for one detail: humans have evolved, and freedom has carved out many imprints in the bedrock of vast eons. Luciferic consciousness is your innate capacity to freely choose. That freedom, at some point, branched into another major artery, known in ancient Persian culture as Ahriman, or in your westernised Christian nomenclature, the Devil or Satan. This part of consciousness not only had freedom, but also chose a particular path motivated by specific inner tendencies.

Now evolution had three major streams: Source, Lucifer and Ahriman. Source itself required a representative in the evolving matrix, and that agency has been named variously as Christ, Yahweh, Allah, Krishna, Brahman, Zeus and innumerable other cultural and religious designations. Source is a better word to avoid particularism, as is the Adversary to denote the Devil. Source and the agency often get confused, but in effect they are the same. What is important to understand is that these two streams of Lucifer and the Adversary are energies that are inter-dimensional and play out in your fourth dimensional environment.

Lucifer especially expresses as a love of freedom. The Adversary especially expresses as a desire to control. Both these forces are not in themselves problematic, if they were faithful servants of Source. But this is where a great divergence has occurred. The Adversary is an outgrowth of Lucifer.

Lucifer was born from the desire of Source to relate to itself from outside. Part of Source desired this separation, and Lucifer was that part, a part that was most precious to Source, a part that was closest to Source in every way.

In freedom, Lucifer desired what Source desired and yet independently, and this could potentially deviate from Source. Lucifer could freely choose to align with Source, or develop along independent avenues. This is how the rays streamed out into both harmonious and disharmonious directions, and one such ray separated itself from Lucifer to a great degree. In freedom, Lucifer allowed a part of itself to separate, a part that was also part of Source, but now further removed than Lucifer, and that part became known as Ahriman, Satan or the Devil. The Adversary was a particular desire different in intensity and type to all other Luciferic desires. This Demonic ray desired to control as Source does. I do not wish to describe the complex evolution of the Luciferic and Demonic rays in detail, but to explain how they are playing through your fourth dimensional situation in this phase of your planetary evolution.

The real question facing humanity is how to bring Lucifer and the Adversary into compliant alignment with Source. To understand this, it is important to acknowledge other powers exist that are essentially aligned with Source. These powers can be simplified into two main streams, those aligned and non-aligned with Source.

Discerning the difference between these two streams is a capacity inherent within souls, but covered over by layers of confusion and illusion. Luciferic energies create confusion with all manner of sensory desire. Demonic energies confuse with lies, illusion and manipulated control. The energies aligned with Source, by contrast, strip away these confused layers, but this is now more difficult than ever, or easier than ever depending on what has been cultivated over many incarnations. This is the time of reckoning. Most human beings are now experiencing both these major streams in mixed degrees, within and without. Many souls have been influenced by both streams, and must discern between them, and this is where choices become important.

No matter what is unfolding on your planet, the greatest challenge is within your own mind and heart. Lucifer and the Adversary are only as powerful as they are allowed to be by each individual. The same applies to those forces aligned with Source. This is where the great work needs to be furthered.

Your choices are omnipresent and accumulative. You are surrounded by vast, confused energies, and you must have simple and powerful ways to counteract them. Anyone can fall into confusion, but this becomes less probable as spiritual practices are merged into daily living.

The world will challenge you. Right now, humanity is passing through an especially challenging phase, and yet this has occurred many, many times before. The energies of desire and manipulated control are everywhere, but you can stand in the storm without losing balance. This is your planetary time of transformation into fifth dimensional universal consciousness. It cannot happen without a great battle.

That battle must be fought inwardly, for the outer battle to succeed. Be aware of the many Source-aligned powerful forces that you can call down into your beings from intergalactic and interstellar realms. Everything essential that is hidden must be revealed. Fourth dimensional consciousness infested by Luciferic and Demonic radiations, as it were, must be cleansed.

One major expression and means through which both Lucifer and the Adversary ply their trade is consumerism. Lucifer traps you via desire for all manner of material objects, from gadgets to houses. The Adversary uses this materialistic trap to control you, and everyone, and everything else. Together they have assumed human leadership, and seem to have achieved their main goals: control over the resources, institutions and life of your planet. But I tell you plainly, this is not the end of the story, far from it.

The successful win over a loser must, by nature, rebalance. They who are first will be last. Those who are last will be first. The pendulum will swing until equilibrium is reached. Equilibrium's swing of arc will be rhythmically narrow. When the arc becomes very wide, extreme consequences ensue. Balance must be interior before becoming exterior. The principle of the pendulum and its arc of swing are true, microcosmically and macrocosmically, and your planetary conflicts are intimately related to this theme. As long as there is a great divide between rich and poor, powerful and powerless, and all other social inequalities, there will be conflict. As long as animals and the general environment is considered as meaningless fodder for out-of-control fourth dimensional appetites, so will there be outbreaks of negative consequences. Lucifer and the Adversary ultimately destroy their own towers of wealth and power, until a true shift begins to occur, and that can happen at any moment because of one omnipresent fact. Source is within Lucifer and the Adversary, and they cannot exist in reality separate from Source. This is the one realisation that can break through fourth dimensional gridlocks.

When Source is consciously acknowledged as real and purposefully oriented, human minds can ask questions never before possible. If I am not in charge, how do I know what to do? If Source is my leader, what would it have me do? But another realisation must follow. Source and I am not separate. What now? How does that change my questioning? In considering fourth dimensional challenges, it is vital to take into account its complexity. Context can change the significance of anything, and is related in meaning to complexity. Everything is interrelated to one degree or another, and even this is more complex than it appears, because everything is inter-dimensionally and multi-dimensionally related.

I bring this to your attention so that you do not too easily make of my words a fixed view of our universe. Having expressed such, I shall add that in order to discover meaning and purpose from within complexity, it is of paramount importance to understand simplicity. It is here that an interface between fourth and fifth dimensional consciousness becomes vital.

Fifth dimensional consciousness is superior to fourth dimensional consciousness, by virtue of its being transcendentally more aligned with Source. Fourth dimensional consciousness becomes transcended by fifth dimensional consciousness, and such a transformational process informs you that a type of sacrifice is necessary.

The way this sacrificial process occurs can vary, but always includes a conscious recognition of fourth dimensional limitation. In other words, thought will acknowledge its own inherent limitation. This, though, is not enough; it is only a step in the process. A practice must be utilised that initiates consciousness into actual experiential change: change that is qualitative and trans-dimensional.

This is where some form of meditation becomes important, but as with all topics of importance there are myriads of fourth dimensional confusions, misunderstandings and superficial interpretations about what meditation is and isn't.

The correct understanding of meditation must include a deep experience of emptiness, spaciousness and freedom. Your fourth dimensional ideas about freedom tend to be versions of your own desires and ambitions. Authentic freedom is only realised when aligned with Source. It is therefore not your individual freedom, as if you are separated from Source. Within freedom there is spaciousness. Fifth dimensional consciousness is not cluttered by attachments to fourth dimensional ideas and beliefs.

One way to transcend the dominance of fourth dimensional consciousness is to practice emptiness meditation. The particular practices of my biographer are of great interest in this regard, belonging as they do to Source-inspired practices of millennial vintage.

I acknowledge that in your epoch, these practices are ways for many to be humbled beyond over-identification with fourth dimensional beliefs. Meditation should be introduced as early as possible into your cultural and educational environments. It is a way of achieving balance between developing ego and natural spiritual capacities.

May these words inspire you to seriously take up some form of meditation, and help you to bridge between fourth dimensional illusions and isolation into cooperative, trusting, creative modes of mutual endeavour.

Blessings.

Epilogue

This biography has no end point. Surely when I decide to reincarnate, the inter-dimensionality that is intrinsic here will undergo a change. My biographer will refocus in other complimentary ways. This present arrangement can continue until the effectiveness is considered better served by superseding shifting dimensions.

It is energetically being asked of me to address specific pressing matters of your present planetary fourth dimensional situation. Once again we enter into complexity, but I will attempt to clarify a few important features. If you focus on a particular event or connected series of events, the first real question you should be asking is, 'What exactly am I witnessing here?' In almost all cases an external event is a symptom, outcome, play-out, externalisation and example of inter-dimensional complexity that make 'getting at' the root causes fraught with difficult challenges. I am happy to focus on one particular event and use it as an example. We can look at this as a case study in complexity, but with an eye on important threads and insights that can emerge.

It has been decided to focus on the Paris suicide attacks that occurred on Friday November 13th 2015. By the time you read this, the energy and fourth dimensional focus, especially through your media outlets, will have diminished, and other events will be the flavour of the day. Nonetheless, the Paris event happened while this biography was being written, and Paris has specific karmic connections to both my biographer and me. It is not my intention to reiterate much that has already been well canvassed by your social media, including some non-mainstream outlets. Rather I wish to probe much deeper into what an occurrence such as the Paris slaughter brings to light when considered from a greater perspective.

Humanity is in reality one planetary species with many sub-streams of evolutional development. These sub-streams have evolved over vast periods of time from a fourth dimensional perspective. The root causes of a single event such as Paris, therefore, belong to a history of ray sub-streams that have their genesis in antiquity and beyond, because these divergent streams didn't originate on your planet, but only developed along particular lines once embodied humanoid breeding programs were initiated. This may seem extremely unrelated, and without present relevance to Paris in 2015, but it is not so. These sub-streams have evolved in uniquely different ways and this diversity in and of itself is not the real problem. What became problematic was that some sub-streams developed in ways that were intrinsically at odds with others. Such deeply disharmonious tendencies could only ever be resolved by an eventual reconciliation of disparate tendencies and often distinct polarities.

What is needing fourth dimensional resolution is to factor in and understand that souls reincarnate. Souls who have not resolved conflict inwardly and relationally bring these conflictual karmic tendencies into rebirths. An entire so-called enemy can be slain, but both victor and vanquished will return to continue their fourth dimensional drama in one form or another. The only real resolution will occur during a particular embodied planetary epoch: in other words in the omnipresent now. This is an evolutionary process. The Paris suicide bombers are souls that became members of ISIS during a particular incarnation. Their inner soul-tendencies, complex as they are, led them to a specific series of choices, and culminated with them believing that by killing others they were doing the right thing. From their perspective what they did was justified. This needs to be understood. If in some, as was actually the case, there was a degree of doubt about the rightness of their actions, it was powerfully overridden by beliefs that they were justified from a larger perspective. This is an example of a universal fact. Luciferic and Demonic consciousness believes in its own 'separated' viewpoint. These consolidated viewpoints are used by powers that are themselves dominated by narrow self-interests. It becomes a messy quagmire of entrapped elements and embodied interpretations, a hellish realm of related destructive tendencies. The question to be pondered is: how did such myopic, unquestioning, rigid viewpoints become established? And how did that play out in the Paris event? And finally, what lessons can present embodied humans learn from this, and what can they do about it? These ways of viewing the world didn't emerge from nothing. Every individual, of course, is an ongoing story in human form. No two stories or human lives are exactly the same.

A major aspect of our individual stories is how particular tendencies and viewpoints solidify over evolutional time. We are attracted to a particular rebirth as a consequence of previous embodiments. The environment we are reborn into is not random, but is intimately part of our individual stories. As souls we are developing according to the complex nature of our core tendencies. This condensed soul nature is influenced strongly by the environment we are reborn into. If you were to follow in reverse the story of a suicide bomber, you would be amazed by the complex threads that make up just one person's story. Some of those threads would touch on universal themes and topics, and it is those that you most need to acknowledge and understand, otherwise you will only ever react to the outermost surface of the event, and nothing useful will be learnt. We must begin to empathise with some of the more common threads, which doesn't mean to excuse an action, but without empathy nothing will change and such events will continue endlessly. Many of these threads are a level deeper than ideology. They are emotional, and underlie ideology and viewpoint. Now the questions can shift. We can ask, 'What are these underlying emotions and what is their genesis?' Naming emotions is a tricky business because different emotions tend to intertwine, but let us loosely name a few that would have been present in most of the Paris suicide bombers to various degrees: resentment, anger, fury, despair, righteousness, pain, trauma, revenge, hate and hope. I have added hope because to kill oneself as well as others in this extreme way is in the false belief that a reward in a higher dimension will be gained. All of these emotions support each other in intricate ways. They all underlie the acceptance of a radicalised version of the world.

The next question must be, 'How did this play out in the Paris event?' The response is obvious if you can penetrate deeply into such emotions. These emotional threads combined to such a degree that minds were possessed by an essentially negative archetype. This is what you must begin to grasp. That negative archetype feels as if it has nothing to lose. It is fighting for its survival in this world or another. It is engaged in what is felt and perceived to be a Holy war or Jihad. In this belief, fuelled by extreme emotions, the enemy is the infidel, and they witness this enemy everywhere in the external fourth dimensional world. It is this view with its underlying emotions that must be understood and empathised with if any chance of a shift in consciousness is to take place. As long as you perceive this as a war, you will strengthen this view in the other. In one sense it is a war, but the real war is within consciousness itself. The jihad is internal and projected externally. If you want to defeat an external enemy, you must understand them and realise where there are common features within yourself. God and the Adversary must learn to dialogue within. Your entire civilisation is an example of warlike personifications essentially embedded within and projected externally.

So how are we to relate to any now deceased Paris suicide bomber? You must begin by understanding him. His story is not separate from yours. Killer and killed belong to the same larger story, we all do, including myself even if I am discarnate. Are you catching a little subtle understanding? I am not intending to disregard in the least the suffering caused by the suicide bombers, but suffering is actually a common link in the larger story. I will focus next on the topic of suffering because this is close to a vital and essential part of what fourth dimensional consciousness has to recognise, reconcile and transform. Before we enter into a discussion about suffering let me make it quite clear: it is your planetary leadership, both political and corporate, that is responsible for the types of suffering that is labelled a 'war on terror.' Paris is only one example of consequences that are related to insane policies that implicate most so-called Western democracies. This is the backdrop of the types of suffering that your world is experiencing in relation to so-called terrorism. This is complex once again, but will be and must be continuously exposed if real change is to occur and future Paris's and 9/11's are to be avoided. The time for truths that have been concealed for years is upon you. The corporate, political, media alliance that has been driven by narrow self interest and insane policy decisions will be exposed. Paris is a victim of human insanity, outlandish greed and stupidity. It will happen again and again until you transform individually and collectively. Revenge is a cover-up reaction that separates the individual from your collective unconscious collusion. You are all partly responsible for what happens. You are all also potential agents of change.

Suffering is itself another complex topic. Firstly, you must distinguish pain from suffering. Pain is a particular type of suffering, but not the type I wish to focus upon. The deeper stratum of human suffering far transcends physical pain. It is within layers of inner sensitivity that are part of your spiritual nature. In relation to Paris, the suffering there is because you are all living, loving, spiritual beings. It is due to such suffering that transformation can happen. The question here is, 'How much suffering needs to happen before major change into fifth dimensional conscious awakening turns your planetary evolution towards harmony and peace?'

Suffering belongs to the fractured relationship between Source and independent agency. Independent agency must accept separation, and therefore glory in the relationship, or return to Source and be no part of an evolving universe. There are two ways to end suffering. For many incarnated souls who are developing and transitioning into fifth dimensional spiritualised embodiments, various involvements with organisations become as bridges. This is now more widespread on your planet than ever before, where a plethora of such organised groups exist. I too was both a member and later founder of an organisation. My biographer has also been engaged with this commonplace array of spiritual organisations with their positive benefits, but also hindrances and pitfalls.

You have a saying, 'No man is an island', and this is intrinsically true. No being is separate from the whole; the universal matrix is your home. A microcosm or fractal of this universal principle is clustering relationships, and then a smaller fractal all inter-personal interactions. Clusters include your fourth dimensional spiritual organisations. In effect they attempt to replicate their intergalactic and interstellar ancestors.

Your spiritual groups are fourth dimensional clusters trying to transition into fifth dimensional collective entities. There are numerous secular attempts too, that by fostering deeper qualities aligned with Source, are spiritual in nature despite how they may be perceived. In the same way, so-called spiritual groups that do not foster qualities aligned with Source are spiritual in name only. In reality your groups, both spiritual and secular are blends of both aligned and non-aligned tendencies and energies.

The organisation I founded as the following of a spiritual impulse has now branched into many sub-streams of activity, some most definitely aligned with Source, or the purpose and vision of Source, and other sub-streams less so. This is inevitable because human souls are at vastly different stages of development and belong to various sub-streams and even rays. Nonetheless, I have some responsibility for the evolutional development of this broad 'church'. I do not mean to suggest that this particular organisation is another religion, but it does have a deeply spiritual foundation, and it is this that must be acknowledged, understood and entered into. Every spoke of a wheel connects to the hub, and each spoke relates to other spokes only as secondary expressions. For the relationship each spoke has with the hub is primary and of paramount importance. Any spiritual organisation must cultivate this two-fold relationship in the correct balance.

When two individual souls have direct fifth dimensional relationship with Source, the secondary but vital fourth dimensional relationship between each other becomes spiritualised too. This is where the vertical and horizontal arms of the sacred cross meet at the fifth central meeting place, and where all multiplicity and duality become sacralised into one great harmony. All distinctions melt into merged Source.

The external expression of this occurs within fourth dimensional human community and culture and spiritual groups are the evolutionary pioneering flagships of this development. Where imbalances occur within such groups, corrective measures can be challenges for individual members. Corrective measures may meet resistances, but such dynamics are always to be expected in your transitional evolutional era.

If you are an agent of corrective change, find others whose relationship with Source essentially echoes your own. Do not compromise by downgrading your own sacred insights and impulses, but be skilful in your patient execution.

Most importantly, do the inner work that external challenges bring to light, as if in a hall of mirrors. Know that this inner-outer work is part of an intergalactic and interstellar evolutional process.

Do not become disheartened or depressed by momentary expressions of fourth dimensional chaos and conflict, such as the Paris bombings, or negative aspects from within any spiritual or secular group you may be involved in.

It is very good that you are so engaged.

Keep on working. Nothing is in vain.

Moment by moment.

Blessings!

Afterword

It is time (an interesting concept in a timeless zone) to pass the mantle on to another working in the same cluster as my biographer and me. This cluster work is vital, and especially important to be increasingly taken up in your incarnated planetary environment. I shall turn my focus to other matters. Parelsitus will be next in line for the biographer to work with. May we all continue to further the evolutional unfoldment towards a glorious and sacred visionary embodiment: an interstellar, intergalactic and earthly celebration of harmony, wisdom and love.

Blessings!

Addendum

Responses to questions from readers of the first edition

This type of multidimensional communication was demonstrated following a meeting with a group of people who had read the first edition and met with the author to discuss their responses. Each had a different point of inquiry and these were used to meditate interdimensionally to generate questions to Elucia. The responses came via the following inspired writing sessions and form the new part of this book.

On Language

It is a self-evident experience that consciousness exists at a deeper level than language. This self-evident experience must be the basis of any investigations into the nature and purpose of language. Eating food is a deeper level of experience than reading a menu. Once having eaten food a description of the experience can be forthcoming. This connects language to experience. We are not talking science here. Scientific methodology doesn't rely on a primary connection of experience and language. It attempts to connect objective testing of phenomena with replicative testing, and only then uses a dissociative language to describe so-called facts. But such use of language does not account for experience. Experience in the present context is subjective. When it is stated that consciousness exists at a deeper level than language, the self-evident truth of this is experientially subjective. Replication of this 'truth' can only be attained by other individuals subjectively claiming the same observation and using the same or equivalent language to describe such an experience. A phenomenological approach to understanding differences between consciousness and language underpins any attempt at asking other questions about the significance of language.

Birds use language too, and if one listens to birds without judgement a sense of something happening beyond mechanical instinct begins to be intuited and perceived. Nature is something more than mechanical. Human experience likewise is a part of nature and non-mechanical. Just because thought, language and actions can be reduced to appear mechanical, does not mean that they are. In essence nature, whether human, earthly or cosmic, has a living consciousness that is subjectively self-evident. It is here that we come upon a barrier. The barrier is of language, but also perception and experience. It must be acknowledged that not all humans have the same experiences. If a claim is made regarding the primacy of experience over language, then this in itself doesn't overcome the problem of subjective differentiation.

What then is meant by the word 'experience?' There are obviously a range of experiences, but there is depth of experience that is not only self-evident but also universal, in other words, common to all. The experience of self existence is one such. This is where the separation between experience and language can become obvious. The I AM presence or consciousness is self-evident but any linguistic description becomes entirely of a lower depth of reality. I know I Am but cannot describe what or who I Am except superficially. The best linguistic descriptions of anything are approximations. Language is limited by its very nature. The I Am example is an intriguing one, and for centuries Buddhists have denied the reality of a self. But this denial is itself a linguistic trap. The mystery of I Am or Selfhood does not imply non-existence. If on the other hand, Buddhist non-self implies that the linguistic descriptions of self are false, then that would be correct. The other challenge that the Buddhist non-self can bring into focus is the idea that self is a separate real entity, but we shall leave that topic alone for now.

We can ask, 'What then is the greater purpose of language, if there is one?' If there is a greater purpose for language it must either be self-created or inspired by a more powerful agency. If it can be inspired by a more powerful agency there are important implications. It also implies that any greater purpose of language would be connected to any purposes a more powerful agency would have. Another implication is that if these conjectures are more than mere speculative theory, a possibility of self-evident experience must be present.

Could the more powerful agency be consciousness? If we accept the premise that consciousness is a greater reality and power than language, we must ask what actually do we mean by consciousness? Scientific materialists believe that consciousness is an epiphenomenon of brain function. The partial truth in this perspective is that consciousness is influenced by its environment, and whatever it is embodied within is a primary part of its environment. But this is a far call from believing that consciousness does not exist beyond the confines of its environment, including the brain. Language in its spoken and written form is obviously dependent on the physical instrument, but this does not exhaust other experiences of language and communication. Consciousness itself exists multidimensionally, and its functioning as strongly influenced by a physical embodiment is only one dimension of many. Any authentic path of spiritual transformation involves degrees of expanding consciousness and openings into multidimensional experience. Expanding multidimensional conscious experience then becomes its own self-evident validation. The question that then ought to be asked is, how does subjective experience become objectively verified? Certainly not by scientific replication in a laboratory. When a number of individuals gather together and share experiences, despite limitations of language, empathy can ensue. Empathy is also multidimensional. At deeper levels of empathy, multidimensional experiences of consciousness can find expression through language. Because language is strongly influenced by cultural norms, when trying to describe experiences that go beyond those norms, language takes on an expanded cultural form.

Consciousness in its purest state is transcendent of all layers of form. In other words, it is empty. The self evident experience of emptiness is the Samadhi of Eastern spiritual traditions. From the perspective of empty consciousness all form is Lila or the 'play of creation' of Godhead. Language such as the preceding words are culturally coloured, and an example of how particular cultural and linguistic forms are filters though which the singular great light of 'Godhead' expresses and manifests. If a soul open-mindedly and open-heartedly spends time in proximity around different cultural, religious and ethnic peoples, commonalities are discovered that transcend externalities.

Communication that connects people at the core depth of human beingness is known as 'satsang' in some Eastern traditions. Empathy at this level can be sublime and profound, akin to falling in love. When we refer to language that aligns with deep Consciousness, we are indicating a synthesis between emptiness and form. The Greeks in classical times spoke of 'the one and the many', not as either/or, but simultaneously. Only a meditation practice can bring a soul into the 'field' of infinite spaciousness and emptiness. Language can then penetrate layers of intellectual reactivity and rest in calm knowing beyond all concepts, and can then, if it chooses, express indicatively and suggestively. Language is the menu or road-map that can penetrate into an experiential self-evident knowing. This was once known as 'gnosis', or core experiential knowledge. Poetry, for instance, has sought to bring winged words to receptive minds. Musical lyrics and music itself has sought too, to penetrate into deeper human experience. Great art and literature have likewise attempted to express the inexpressible. As a reflective process self-expression can lead to insights. Reflective consciousness implies a capacity to reflect thoughtfully on what is thought and expressed.

There is another key element involved in the use of language: that of intention. Intention changes context. Two individuals may be walking along the same avenue but with different destinations. What is the purpose of language at any given moment? What is the intention behind the words? This investigation again and again leads back to the need for clarity of consciousness. The prime intention within this chapter is for consciousness to awaken to its core state of empty awareness and to inspire others to explore meditation and transformational dialogue.

On Identity

Imagine a tapered funnel, very narrow at one end and broad at the other. The entire funnel represents a specific faculty of human consciousness, namely that of 'identity'. I wish to share with you a perspective of identity that can transform your inner life, and most probably your outer life too.

The narrow end of the funnel is indicative of degrees of boredom and boring. Boredom for many is unconscious. It has become the norm. There is a cause for chronic unconscious boredom and there are also numerous symptoms. Identity at the narrow end of the funnel can be chronically bored because of its superficial and minuscule understanding. The dominating experience at the narrow end of the spectrum tends to be intellectual, conceptual and narcissistic. Consciousness has been gradually funnelled into a micro-spheric contraction, consisting of name, personal biography, status and inherited beliefs. If identity is totally limited to a micro-spherical orb it will be felt that one's separated self with all its habits and perceptions are essentially the fundamental reality. The question, 'Who am I?' can then only be responded to in a limited way. For instance, I am my body, thoughts and emotions. In other words, I am whatever my conditioned beliefs are.

We can imagine passing further into the funnel towards the wider end. This is when a soul begins to question whether the little orb of personal identity is all there is. It may be a confusing phase. A relatively fixed sense of identity can afford a type of illusory security. Boring and bored can be the price for such an illusion of security. Soul is more than body, mind and emotion. The narrower end of the funnel represents individuality and is perfectly accountable as a 'part' of who a person is. But it is no more the whole person as are the surface waves of the ocean.

As we observe the wider middle part of the funnel we enter the realm of 'feeling'. This is the realm of the fourth dimension, yet influenced by third dimensional biological instincts. The fifth dimensional pull forward moves into conflict with third dimension past gravitas. Identity within the fourth dimension undergoes a disturbance as it shifts from rigid materialism towards an etheric flow wave. In other words, feelings and senses begin to mutate as an evolutionary process.

The physical organism undergoes subtle changes too, as it always has done when evolutionary quantum shifts occur.

It is also within the middle section of our symbolic funnel that identity itself undergoes an experiential mutation. 'Who am I?' now cannot be easily responded to. There is a growing intuition and sensory 'feeling' that one's identity is a mystery beyond the outmoded narrow view of yesteryear. Esoteric teachings can now come within the orbit of intuitive comprehension. A new inner organ is being nurtured into being. Intellect begins to serve etheric sensitivity, and if faculties and qualities of consciousness are reasonably fine tuned, an integration of third, fourth and fifth dimensions develops.

As soul passes into the wide end of the funnel, a monumental shift begins to occur, reminiscent of an emerging butterfly. Identity now shifts beyond all conceptual and intellectual images and ideas into a sense of unbounded vastness. For this shift to be humanely safe, all dimensions need to be balanced. The entire funnel must be activated as a single integrated organism. Identity now can move in and out of infinite space. This is the meaning behind seeming riddle-like paradoxes such as 'you are someone and no one simultaneously.'

We must now re-enter the middle of the funnel again, for it is here that our intellect can be engaged in a radically new way. Soul is now stirring: awakening to its own latent potential. This shift along the funnel is no simple jaunt. Intellect has developed extraordinarily into physical and material identification. The antidote to this over-identification with materialism is at least partly a development and cultivated refinement of language.

Language must speak to the soul. It must awaken soul faculties. Soul must experience itself as self-evident. Words must be winged messengers from spiritual realms. But intellect must also be appeased. The entire funnel must become as a harmonious symphony. Identity must become transfigured into a mystical transparency. Meditative consciousness must become a consistent hub of being. When soul crosses thresholds into expanded consciousness it can bring back to intellect and language some spirit treasures. Indeed language, both written and spoken, must bring soul-awakening magic into fields of ordinary everydayness. Sublime must meet mundane and enlighten it. Identity must surrender its narrow intellectual stranglehold and be re-birthed.

Soul will begin to perceive the intellectual layer of self as an object rather than the subject. In other words, observation will become increasingly objective. The soul behind thoughts will be perceived self-vidently as a greater reality than the thoughts themselves. This will be as a portal into deep inner spaces of peace and silence. An entire reformed outer culture could be manifested from this profound inner reality. It begins with each moment of immersion into sacred spaces and its outer engagement with the world of form.

This sacred dance is a qualitative movement that is the very essence of living art. The funnel of multidimensional self becomes a celebration of unity, harmony and bliss. Identity has shattered its illusory shells and breathes the sanctified atmosphere of freedom.

At the heart of this transformation is meditative consciousness. It cannot be otherwise. To be in the world yet not of it is the great challenge facing individuals, communities and humanity at this historical threshold. It is a massive balancing act. You are bombarded by tempting sensory stimuli. Thought and perception are attracted this way and that. You get caught in webs of microscopic details. You are the tragic or comic stars of your own soap operas. Of course the range of mind-created images within this whirlpool of social stimuli is vast, but all flotsam and jetsam on the ocean's surface. Without a way into a deeper, vaster realm, this plateau becomes a hypnotic crystallised coma. Naturally, from an ordinary perspective social and personal dramas can be experienced as the norm.

A caterpillar doesn't miss being a butterfly. One might imagine though, as the caterpillar nears its stage of retreating into a cocoon, there may be some mysterious, indefinable inner feeling, an intuition that there is more to existence than remaining a caterpillar. Then there is an incubation phase. Likewise souls ready for a transition from fourth to fifth dimensional consciousness must undergo transformation. A caterpillar identity is an effective metaphor for souls yet unable to perceive their potential greater identity. Butterflies know how it is to be more than they were. Spiritually awakened souls know too what it is like to be more than what they were. They are experiencing it!

On Awakening

If a soul surrenders conditioned intellectual reasoning and, so to speak, drops into deeper realms of feeling, an awakening can happen: immediately. This can be a qualitative sudden shift in consciousness, or a wake-up call.

Human experience tends to get stuck in cul-de-sacs. Souls have outlived their evolutionary usefulness and many yearn for a way out of an experiential entrapment. In your recent history, increasing numbers of souls have reincarnated with a deep hunger for experiences that general culture denies them. This leads to various forms of personal and collective upheaval and deformity. Culturally ingrained forms of conservative crystallisation prohibit and discourage souls from developing naturally creative gifts. This has arisen from an evolutionary disturbance ancient in origin. Even prior to what can be more easily perceived, there is a cause that derives from Godhead itself. We must remind ourselves that our universe is predicated upon a core principle: that of freedom. Freedom is an active principle, meaning that it creates. Creativity has no meaning if it doesn't contain a degree of freedom.

The long march of evolution has led to the miraculous life on your planet. Human beings are the apex of this wondrous cosmic theatre. But growth of human faculties, especially intellect, have outgrown a moral imperative. There is a great need now for awakenings of soul and consciousness. This implies the establishment of rites of passage. A rite of passage is a qualitative shift that naturally transforms consciousness, perception and understanding. It is a maturation of soul. It should not be forced but rather aided and encouraged. If encouraged, souls would pass through natural rites of passage. Thwarted rites of passage become maladies of frustration, anxiety, fear, unnatural conformity and existential boredom. Narcotic substances and other addictions offer escapisms, compensations and sometimes chemically induced awakenings, but warped, as they are unintegrated and therefore dangerous for soul and community. If culture generally lacks wise foundational processes that would provide natural and safe rites of passage, then how is a soul to cross over great thresholds?

The essential reality underpinning awakening is an existential truism that can be expressed as 'The soul within the machine'. In other words, the I AM in its omnipresent primacy can be conscious of itself at any given moment. This soul-self recognition is an awakening of soul to itself: the I AM That I AM on a soul level of identity. This in itself may change nothing, other than elicit a passive epiphany, or it can be a catalyst for transformational change. When time-related processes or incremental changes are combined with sudden awakenings, a potent activation can be set in motion. Meditative in-turnings that bring about awakenings are vital for such a spiritually-aware life.

The recognition of the personal I AM is also a portal into the cosmic I AM. Consciousness is active at both a soul and spirit depth, with this distinction referring to different perspectives of a single reality. Therefore the I AM is simultaneously Christ consciousness and God consciousness filtered through the funnel of human potential into self-created thoughts, images and beliefs. The simple act of I AM self-recognition can bring about an immediate awakening. I AM in its uttermost simplicity and purity is transcendent of all thought and form. It is a primal state of unhindered cosmic awareness, empty in itself and the creator of all that issues forth. The I AM is free to choose. It is then possible to assume soul-control of thought. 'Soul in the machine' then regains leadership. Machine in this context is a metaphor for thought. Soul guided by divine impulses can gradually assume consensual leadership of all human faculties.

What is communicated above must acknowledge the role soul clusters, or groups of souls, play in the progression along spiritual paths. Breaking out of illusory isolation opens a receptive soul to collaborations that otherwise would be impossible. Breaking free of limited linear and materialistic thinking opens a soul to inter-dimensional communications beyond ordinary limited consciousness. It can be difficult to burst the bubble of limited materialistic and sensory-influenced thinking. Dialogue is a way to share experiences which fall outside of normal social norms. Indeed, there is a great need for new types of language and other artistic creativity. No one can claim the one golden way. We souls, both incarnate and discarnate, are caught in one complex matrix. We must gradually awaken together, in freedom.

On Christ

You want me to communicate about Christ in a contemporary manner: in a new language and from a discarnate perspective that is freer than when I was embodied. The confusion existing between the distinctly different dimensions of Christ and Jesus has been and is in dire need of clarity. A relationship between these two dimensions as a prototype for all humanity was exemplified by what transpired a little over two thousand years ago. It wasn't the first occurrence of this merging of dimensions, but the manner of its unfolding brought a new impulse into terrestrial evolution.

Christ is the active expression of Godhead. In order for Christ to incarnate, a suitable vehicle must be prepared. This preparation is the great secret of evolution. It is the original divine impulse. When the original separation took place, the singularity of Godhead became dispersed. This dispersion is mythically depicted as Christ and Lucifer, and later Ahriman.

These classifications are indicators. Their reality is only truly understood when contemplative and meditative in-turnings reveal experiential micro-spheric insights. Christ must be realised as the Godhead in its active faculty. This implies firstly consciousness of the Godhead as manifested by Christ. Without Christ, the Godhead would have no objective reality. Jesus was a human being who received the Christ impulse and realised the transcendent at-one-ness of 'Father and Son.' This patriarchal mythos can be also expressed as 'Mother and Son.' For contemporary understanding, these differing mythic figures should be flexibly related to, because what is being revealed is archetypal. In other words, it is an axiom that transcends limited language.

Jesus as a person living two thousand years ago needs to be understood in historical terms. His own relationship with Christ needs to be understood within an historical context. Historical also implies a hidden evolutionary dimension. History is the unfolding of evolutionary impulses in all their multidimensional complexity. At the time of Jesus in the Middle East and Near East, there was a cultural and religious mix in place that had become politicised and antagonistic. Factions of every type co-existed but mostly in ways that confounded attempts to establish harmony and, even more significantly, to foster wisdom, clarity and love. Those individuals and groups who moved away from social confusion and bigotry mainly formed communes away from the hustle and bustle of the crowded cities. The Essenes were one such community. There was no over-riding or underlining philosophy or religious core able to hold the numerous factions together in cohesive co-existence. The ruling classes held sway, and Judaism had fossilised into dogma and ritualistic myopia. The legacy of this 'blind leading the blind' cultural and religious environment has continued in various forms and is still prevalent in your world today. But Jesus as a soul belonged to a soul cluster of profound spiritual and historical significance and heritage.

To understand the deeper import of Jesus and his relationship to Christ, it is vital to realise that there has always been a soul-cluster especially focused on the evolutional imperative of merging Godhead with human consciousness and then into cultural and spiritual embodied living.

The orientation towards a fulfilment of the divine vision emanating from Godhead, of a fully merged spiritual Human, has needed quantum shifts to occur within cultural and religious environments, if human evolution was not to self implode and abort its evolutional potential and purpose.

Such quantum shifts operating through specially prepared individuals can be viewed as divine intervention, but really they are super-natural or supra-natural evolutional events. In other words, they are supremely natural but beyond nature in its physical dimension. Such individuals and events are harbingers of, and belong to a Christ impulse. What does this mean? It reveals that behind the screen of history and evolution there is an impulse directly emanating from Godhead. This impulse is the intention and inner vision of Godhead dispersing into numerous rays of externalisation as depicted in my previous communications. Consciousness that belongs to and is inseparable from Godhead is what is known by you as Christ.

Rays belonging to the remembrance of 'Christ Consciousness' belong to a different group of rays to those that forgot their origin in order to develop along other evolutional directions. Lucifer, for example, was the ego-head of the impulse of individuality. This impulse belonged in truth to the Godhead, because Godhead allowed the ego-head impulse or Luciferic impulse to evolve alongside the Christ impulse. Why? In order for an eventual merging of individuality with Godhead to occur.

Christ is the active agent of Godhead. Human light born of divine light, connecting Godhead to individuality. Jesus understood this. This was his revelation. He had been prepared to receive the Christ impulse and merge with it so fully that he became the natural harbinger of revelation. The events within the life ministry of Jesus needed to be omnipotent (all-powerful) in such a way that the natural evolutional and historical processes received a quantum jolt and shift. Christ needed a foothold in the borderlands between East and West that Arabia was, that would bring a new orientation into existence.

Judaism as the main religious force other than the older religions of the Orient, such as Hinduism, Taoism and Buddhism, needed to be challenged. Judaism, as Mosaic law, had become bogged down in externalities and hierarchical privilege. It had lost its universality. Christianity was to follow suit in many ways, but a new catholic (universal) impulse was needed. Jesus was a universalist. He knew with his inner vision that Godhead was the source of all life. He knew Christ as the active agency of Godhead existing within the consciousness and being of every human being and unconsciously within all living creatures.

His mission on Earth was to be totally dedicated to the awakening of Christ within the souls he encountered. He had been Christened or Christed and now accepted his role as prepared vehicle for an evolutional and historical mission. The Mystery of Golgotha is a mystery in so far as the historical story hides the greater significance of the event. Jesus chose to be crucified as a message to all humanity that there is no greater human action than to live for the merger of Christ and human. Through Christ, Godhead is made flesh and the separation of Christ from flesh is merely a temporary appearance. Jesus chose consciously the most extreme example of dedication to Christ and the Christ impulse by allowing his mortal human self to be degraded, humiliated and crucified.

It was asked why not much was transmitted in Elucia about Christ. May this be a part response to that question. If it evokes further questions, so be it. I only respond to questions whether consciously recognised or somewhat veiled behind other superficial questions.

On Technology

The invention of the wheel was a technological breakthrough. Before that, harnessing fire was a tremendous evolutionary leap forward. Domesticating animals and cultivating crops so they can be utilised to ease labour needs were other technological advances. Modern people tend not to regard these changes in human evolutionary development as technological, but they are in the most essential sense of the word. And it within this context that the most important point needs to be made; that it is the human factor that is important rather than the technology itself. Every one of those examples above have been used for good and evil. Think about that.

It is exactly the same as the ever-changing development of modern technologies. The human factor is the relevant factor. It is obvious that the machine doesn't rule the human. People think up ideas and those ideas sometimes materialise. When they do manifest and take root as a part of popular culture, the human motivation becomes the driving force. The machine doesn't choose how and why it is utilised.

If you seriously and deeply contemplate a simple situation, such as the invention of the wheel, you can imagine (as an exercise) how it could be used for both good and evil. Now with wheels you can be more mobile. You can invent a chariot or a cart. You can combine this with another potentially great invention: the domestication and breeding of horses. Now what will you do with this combined leap forward in technology? And how will you educate your children and influence your community in the uses of these wondrous new developments in human cultural evolution?

What has changed over millennia? Only the extent of the effects and consequences that the uses of technology have. And this is a very significant 'change.' Because the technologies have reached a tipping point in potential effects and consequences. The human factor is largely the same essentially: the freedom to choose why and how to use any technology. But the technologies have developed into ever increasing manifestations of 'power'.

Technology has become very powerful. Think of the difference in 'power of effect' between using a sword, gun and bomb. Behind the use of all three is a human but the power of the weapon becomes increasingly lethal if used malevolently.

So, my friends, you who are presently incarnated continue the legacy of human development alongside that of the technologies you have created. The focus has to be on human transformation. Only then will technology become a constructive adjunct to human culture.

Whatever enhances human transformation from third dimension biological nature into fourth dimension intellectualism and then most importantly into fifth dimension spirituality then contributes towards the safer and healthier uses of technology.

This transformational process is complex and not easily achieved but is at the very foundation of your life missions. The particular focus on the inevitability of advancing technologies including bio-technology simply means that the human factor becomes increasingly significant.

On the Etheric Christ

What can be said about the second coming of Christ? It has already happened. The etheric Christ is among you. It is your own awakened or awakening consciousness. It is the downflow of Christ from mind to feeling to will. It is only when a descent into darkness occurs that light can become stronger. The Christ impulse must soak into earth. It does this multidimensionally. In human affairs it takes place when the earth element is most under threat.

Awakening must take place within the body and all the physical senses must be immersed into the dark earth. Light must penetrate into the darkest places otherwise darkness will be trapped and without redemption. What does it mean that the physical senses must be immersed into the dark earth? The body of humanity is part of the physical dimension and manifestation of existence. A human body is a part of nature, and for nature to be redeemed it must undergo a transformation.

The consciousness within a body, the I AM, is the mediator between spirit and matter. The I AM consciousness is the individuated Christ (the second coming), and must with all its sensory faculties immerse into materialism in order to free it from a self-imposed separation. Individuality must be redeemed from its isolated condition. The words 'dark earth' is a metaphorical expression for the densest materialism that exists, and cannot be avoided in the march of evolution towards the reborn Christed individual.

An example so prevalent in your twenty-first century world is the exponential expansion of technology. Without the I AM Christed consciousness redeeming technology from its own Frankensteinian monstrous orientations, that are unspiritual to one degree or another, a hellish world outcome will be inevitable. On the other hand, if the awakened I AM immerses itself into technology and brings it into the service of the evolutional transformation of humanity and the cosmos, then the Age of Kali Yuga can be brought into the supernal externalised light of spiritual vision and purpose: the Shambala of Godhead's vision and Christ's mission. This immersing into the dark earth is especially important in the field of bio-technology. The immersion cannot be avoided. The splitting of the atom cannot be reversed. The dark earth must be redeemed.

How can we understand and what has become of the new faculties required for perceiving the etheric or risen Christ? These faculties have been largely immersed into the dark earth of materialism and technology. They are existing but, so to speak, submerged. What will bring them forth into consciousness? Only when the faculties become conscious (self aware) can the etheric Christ be perceived. Increasing numbers of human beings are realising the harmful effects of spiritually-unregulated materialism and technology and this removes layers upon layers of energy. If self-willing acts intelligently, leading to an eventual opening of spiritual faculties of consciousness, it then allows for an epiphany of sudden etheric Christ perception. Technology itself is an externalisation of inner evolutionary processes and as with Uroborus, the snake that swallows its own tail, must complete the cycle that reconnects to its origin, the Godhead.

Let me phrase this another way. The ego-head or individualism of the I AM must, through its own creative manifestations, reconnect to the Godhead of which it owes its existence. Only then do we have a true harmony of the spheres. This must be realised deeply inwardly, beyond the indicative words and into a heart vision that is embedded within the soul memory of humanity. This is a meditation, not a university lecture.

Do you have any advice about introducing technology to students?

You cannot isolate students from technology but you can guide them into good uses of it. But really this belongs to a greater topic. Education itself is being challenged to transform its processes. Education should not rely on forms of teaching and curriculum content that are outmoded and essentially irrelevant in a vastly changing environment. This is a complex topic as the Ahrimanic forces of over-regulation have their own agendas driven by particular self interests, many of which are of a non-spiritual nature. Technology could be introduced to students gradually within a larger context. A question for you:

What new topics could be introduced to students that would help to channel their use of technology in creative and positive ways? A particular soul helped me to become more sharply aware of the importance of 'pure observation' and it's relevance to creativity. He did this especially by way of his insights into the pure observation of nature. This influence on my soul did not occur arbitrarily. It helped me to observe the macro within the micro. Christ itself can be perceived as both macro and micro. It is possible to perceive Christ in a wild flower or in the cosmos. Christ is the animating* principle in both the tiniest and greatest of phenomena.(*The word 'animate' as in the sense of Latin 'animatus', to give life to, from 'anima' breath, soul; akin to old English, 'Othian' to breathe, Latin 'animus' spirit, or Sanskrit 'aniti' he breathes.)

Nature in its multifarious abundance and variety offers a visual portal into the animating power of Christ and therefore of the Godhead. Human nature too can be perceived as the creative handiwork and animating principle of both the Godhead and Christ, but Christ is the outpouring of what within the Godhead is only envisioned. The practice of pure observation is then a meditative process that can shift perception in evolutionarily significant ways. When I encountered this particular soul's writings on pure observation within my previous incarnation, it was as if a great window opened, and with it vast waves of fresh illumination. I brought to this newly empowered faculty of observation my own developed faculty of penetrating inward reflection. This in turn helped to bring me to the threshold of Christ consciousness. The I AM, or pure essence of soul, became known as Christ in its individuated form but simultaneously a part of the cosmic I AM that belongs to the Godhead in its singular at-one-ness.

It is the Christ as the animating and activating principle of Godhead, and the drama that is the life of Jesus, that I bring to the soul that revealed the importance of pure observation to me, as shared gifts borne from the sacred collaboration that bears the stamp of our karmic relationship. This is now shared with mutual gratitude. It is the vital importance of experiencing Godhead as empty consciousness that the author brings to this collaboration. This is the union of essence and substance, Godhead and Christ. The I AM is Godhead, Christos and Ego. They are varied dimensions of one reality, similar to different depths of an ocean. The surface, middle and bottom are all part of one ocean. Most humans identify with the surface, with the personal ego. It must be emphasised that all these linguistic derivations and classifications are pointers to 'that' which needs to be experienced. Christ is a word-symbol indicating an experiential phenomena, universal in nature. When the ego-mind recognises this experience in its universality beyond the surface of theory or belief, an awakening or epiphany occurs that shifts consciousness itself. Such a shift is potentially omnipresent. In other words, consciousness is largely asleep in its ordinary state.

What I alluded to in my previous incarnation as a 'second coming of Christ' between 1930 and 1943 needs to be now clarified. This of course was prophetic, but open to many misunderstandings. It needs to be acknowledged that the focus on specific years, in a prophetic context, was never my main concern, and others who then connect what I've once said in lectures to mathematical calculations and other so-called esoteric interpretations, 'after the fact' and after my passing through the gate of death, greatly distort my intentions. Having said as much, there is a significance regarding the years 1930 to 1943, regardless of how those years have been plucked out for special consideration in relation to the second coming of Christ, and his appearance to many as an etheric experience. More can be transmitted about this but first the following historical data should be stated. The rise of national socialism in Germany culminated a series of increasingly nationalistic movements that had become especially virulent since the early 1800's. The French Revolution gave way to Napoleon's rise. In turn this brought the German principalities together and led to a unified Germany. This in turn led to various forms of German patriotism, exacerbated by defeat in the First World War and the consequent Versailles treaty. I perceived in these historical developments a deeper descending into darkness, into the underworld of unconsciousness and brutality that paradoxically would call forth a new wave of awakened consciousness. It is only when human consciousness descends into direst darkness that light is constellated and empowered. It isn't easily realised how in human degradation and cruelty, an embodied experience occurs that transcends belief and all mental activity.

It is this descending into a physical and sensory dominated realm that gives rise to new waves of spiritual awakening. Any descent into material, physical and sensory experience reaches a turning point in consciousness. I foresaw this turn-about happening in the early 1930's. The year 1943 was the year Germany began to lose the war. The external shift paralleled an inner one. There was a growing realisation of the futility of war, largely brought about by a horrendous loss of life and destruction of every type.

It must be understood then that the second coming of Christ does not mean a collective fully conscious awakening. It means a quantum shift in collective consciousness, but a shift that grows and spreads gradually over many decades. Any perceptive overview of recent world history will reveal something about what I'm conveying, beyond doubt. The actual shift had its roots during the darkest years of world history. Do you realise that if German and Japanese militarism had succeeded in ruling world affairs, the world as you know it would never have happened? Imagine what type of world you would now inhabit if Germany, Italy, Japan and Franco's Spain had succeeded in winning and forming a coalition, or warring amongst themselves? Either way the world would have descended into an unimaginable barbaric chaos. This didn't happen for reasons that were anything but random.

Gradually and incrementally a crucified Europe and world resurrected itself, but would never be the same again. Europe especially from 1930 was tortured, defiled and reduced to ashes. Unspeakable events paralleled the events that happened two thousand years earlier. It is interesting to note that Adolf Hitler came to power in 1933, three years after the start of my thirteen year prophesy. Jesus's awakened ministry lasted for three years. One could say that the Fuhrer's Ascension matched the Mystery of Golgotha. The darkest event allows increased light to shine. Light is brighter the greater the darkness.

A question remains: will there be a third coming of Christ? And a fourth and so on? Yes there will be, but the second coming is barely discernible in your present world. The so-called 'New Age' is only one of an evolutional series of 'New Ages.'

Quantum shifts of consciousness are part of your universe's natural evolutional trajectory. The omnipotent, omniscient and omnipresent consciousness of Godhead and Christ in its active movement awaits the human ego development to fulfil Godhead's vision and purpose. For this to complete, a fully embodied ego consciousness must fully merge with Christ and Godhead.

It also needs to be clarified that by the term Christ, Christianity as a religion is not intended. Nor did the historical Jesus found a new religion. Christ is a symbol for universal consciousness. To realise and experience this is to 'be Christed or Christened' in its true context. When Jesus was christened by John in the River Jordan, he suddenly became aware of his divine origin. His sense of a separate (Jewish) identity was superseded and subsumed. A process that had been underway for many years reached its apex. He had been Christed! He was Jesus the Christ. The second coming is when masses of people become Christed: any people, no matter how this is described.

What happened on the hill of Golgotha represented a prototype of what was to happen two thousand years later for many people. I described this in other more abstract terms previously in this book. It was a collaborative attempt to create a more accessible language. But because I didn't often use the word 'Christ', it seemed to some that I ignored this fundamental part of my past teachings. Truth is not static. This is a never ending epic. As such new questions will always arise. But remember, consciousness in its pure state is identical to Godhead, and Godhead is essentially unchanging. I am not concerned with the precise timing of events. Of course, there are micro-macro connections that are significant, and yes, I did often not only become aware of such but also shared information in many of my lectures. But the esoteric meaning of the second coming of Christ as an etheric phenomenon needs freedom to breathe. A soul desiring to understand what this experience is must develop faculties of perception rather than intellectualise about such matters. Even though I can acknowledge a special significance with specific years, to overly focus on this level of information can be 'not seeing the forest for the trees.' Christ as an etheric experience and perception is entirely subjective and it cannot be otherwise.

The 1930's were indeed a descending into collective darkness for Europe, and then, like a virus, the entire world. Within this collective dark night of the soul, the etheric Christ came closer than ever to many. This continues to happen. The Christ genii is out of the bottle, so to speak. I pointed out a special significance of the year 1943 as a way of responding to a question. It should be noted that many of my Jewish followers were killed at that time in concentration camps. 1943 was the year that the Third Reich began to panic, if subconsciously for many involved. There were many other years that could be especially focused upon and connections with a greater spiritual perspective brought into focus: such as 1933. But together as a soul cluster concerned with the evolution of consciousness, and desiring a true meaning of the second coming of Christ, it behoves us to not get overly bogged down in details. We are concerned, whether embodied or not, with the evolution of consciousness. We are collaborating as a soul cluster. We are not competing against each other out of subjective personal choices of ways of expressing that which belongs to a common field of heart truth.

The bringing together of the universal and the particular always presents challenges. My words, filtered as they are through different finite minds, must not be considered as a new gospel. It is not my imagined authority at stake. Christ is beyond all such personal favouritism. If we are to join in collective understanding, a surrendering of the personal must occur. This is a transcendental experience that can bring light into the darkness of over-subjectivity.

I said that the experience of the etheric Christ is of necessity a subjective experience, but the Godhead is not of that order. Godhead is a presence of oneness that transcends all subjective individuality. Then Godhead joins with Christ in Union. This union is known as yoking the Absolute with the transient. In Eastern esoteric tradition the word 'yoke' gave rise to Yoga. All these words are pointers to experiences that rely on developed and developing faculties, and as a soul cluster we are processing together as friends on the path of evolving consciousness. Christ Jesus revealed an esoteric rite of passage on the hill of Golgotha. It is this rite of passage that now can be experienced both personally and collectively. This collective transformation and transfiguration is what the second coming of Christ is about.

The third coming of Christ will be concerned with a physical transformation. That is not of present concern. Humanity is in transition between the fourth and fifth dimensions. A keynote of this transitional epoch is the need for clear dialogue, including vertical exchanges. In other words, Godhead, Christ, incarnated I AM and intellectual ego need to discover and create clear avenues of exchanging information. Dialogue must become refined and alive. Language must become flexible. Consciousness must become settled in pure observation and periods of intentional silence. Godhead is dependent on Christ. Christ is dependent on incarnated individuality. Incarnated individuality (soul) is dependent on intellectual ego. And, I would add, intellectual ego is dependent on education. These can be referred to as interdependent dimensions of universal consciousness. This can be envisaged as a mandala, with Godhead as the singularity in the Center. Each layer around the Center becomes more sophisticated and complex. And yet the whole mandala is a single entity, made up of many parts, simultaneously. For the whole mandala to maintain integrity and cohesiveness, it must not fragment into chaos. This is a matter of clear communication between the dimensions and parts. It is a metaphor for existence.

The nature of your universe is essentially a mandala. Godhead is the centre of the universe. It is existential singularity. The first dimension circling around the Godhead is Christ. Not the Christian Christ, but the Cosmic Christ. The Cosmic Christ is the active principle of Godhead. The 'Word' is consciousness capable of recognising itself. It is original sound and emanation of light and heat. The Cosmic Christ is the pure I AM consciousness. It Is therefore I AM. Godhead Is therefore I AM. This is the mystical revelation of Godhead through Christ. Christ incarnates into human individuality. This is then a trinity. Godhead through Christ into human individuality.

Intellectuality is a conscious embodied faculty that uses 'language' to express in ever more sophisticated and complex forms. The evolutional challenge is to bring into unity these four dimensions. Language and its capacity to create ingenious symbolic systems, such as mathematics, sacred geometry, art, philosophy, psychology, politics, imagination (fiction), games and all other mind-created layers of human expression, is a link to the trinity of I AM ego, Christ and Godhead. The second coming of Christ in the context of 'inter-dimensional' dialogue is thus dependent on increasing faculties and qualities of clear communication and the development of latent faculties transcending mere intellectualism. Intellect understood in this larger context of multidimensionality is a layer of reality corresponding to the clothes we wear. Intellect is the outermost layer of universal conscious reality.

The second coming is about a quantum shift into deeper layers of reality, especially the recognition of the etheric Christ. The etheric Christ is a non-physical insight into the nature of Christ or Christos. It is an inner perception of the reality of Christ as a universal I AM and yet it needs the personal I AM or soul to fully recognise this. All levels of cosmic unfoldment are necessary to engage in this transformative harmonisation. The ultimate expression of reality is: You are intellect, soul, Christ and Godhead!

Other books by Keith Simons:

Quest: A Mystical Autobiography (2004)

Portal: Awakening to Being (2009)

Autobiography of a Russian Yogi (2017)

Poetica Esoterica (2019)

www.ingramcontent.com/pod-product-compliance
Lightning Source LLC
Chambersburg PA
CBHW020649300426
44112CB00007B/309